641.8653
R394
2012

FOND DU LAC PUBLIC LIBRARY

WITHDRAWN

AUG 27 2012

Vintage Cakes

Vintage Cakes

Timeless Recipes for Cupcakes, Flips, Rolls,
Layer, Angel, Bundt, Chiffon, and Icebox Cakes
for Today's Sweet Tooth

Julie Richardson

Photography by ERIN KUNKEL

TEN SPEED PRESS

Berkeley

For all my grandmothers.

And for Hazel, who stuck with me
every step of the way and was always ready
when a chance morsel fell to the floor.

ACKNOWLEDGMENTS

A deep thanks to the wonderful folks of Baker & Spice Bakery and SweetWares, for your support and patience while I took time away from the bakery to work in my home kitchen. Thanks too for your honest critique of the many cakes that found their way to the break table. Kathy High, thank you for your contributions to this book. And an extra special thanks to Ashley Claybaugh and Kelly Smith for keeping things running smoothly in my absence—you both are positively super duper!

I am forever grateful to my recipe testing/tasting team, who were never afraid to say it like it is: Julie Beeler, Karolyn Cross, Gina Fleschner, Laura Gordon, Nellie Hester, Kathie Newbie, Beatrice Pickett, Marguerite Rogers, Barbara Slaughter, Barbara Stollberg, and Lamar White.

A thousand thanks to my dear friend Joy Ellis for helping me pull this book together and bring some order to the stacks of yellow notepads that have littered my kitchen for the past year.

To the amazing people at Ten Speed who honored me with the concept of *Vintage Cakes*, I offer my sincerest gratitude for trusting me to create the book that you envisioned. Special thanks to Jenny Wapner for her insightful editing, Toni Tajima for her inspired design, and to Ethel Brennan and Robyn Valarik for their vintage styling. Erin Kunkel, you are a true talent! Thanks for sharing your gift of photography with *Vintage Cakes*.

Finally, this book could never have happened without one person in particular who washed all my dirty dishes, tasted all my trials and errors, went to the store on a moment's notice for a forgotten ingredient, and made me wholesome meals to offset all that butter, sugar, and flour we consumed on a daily basis as these recipes took shape. Matt, you are without a doubt the sweetest part of my life! Thank you for always believing in me.

I am blessed to be surrounded and supported by my family, friends, and fellow baking allies . . . thank you all for unknowingly contributing to my work.

Contents

INTRODUCTION

Some people's obsessions lead them to mountaintops or shoe stores or the racetrack. Mine led me straight to the kitchen. I am a baker. It's my passion; it's who I am and what I do. I recognized at an early age the thrill of transforming a few simple everyday ingredients (butter, flour, sugar, eggs) into a delicious creation. This joy is what gets me up in the wee hours of the morning to begin my baking day. I have had the pleasure of owning two small neighborhood bakeries in my career, one in Ketchum, Idaho, and my current endeavor in Portland, Oregon.

When we moved into the space in Portland that is now Baker & Spice Bakery, it had already housed a bakery (the Hillsdale Pastry Shop) for fifty years. In the rush of trying to remodel the space and establish a new business, I hastily dumped the contents of one of their old filing cabinets into a sturdy apple box and pushed it into an empty corner of the attic above the bakery.

Once we were settled in, and after fielding a lot of requests for "pink champagne cake" from customers devoted to the previous bakery who apparently missed their favorite dessert, I remembered the box in the attic and decided to take it out and see if it contained any recipes. What I found was a vintage junkie's dream! The history that poured out of that box sent me back in time. It held a gold mine of baking formulas, journals, and magazines dating back to the 1920s. These were gems from a time when a cupcake was a "cup cake," a cookie was a "cooky," and the word "goober" was synonymous with peanut. Bundt pans were still unceremoniously called metal tube pans, and coconut (spelled "cocoanut"), pineapple, and banana were considered exotic ingredients. Housewives were disciples of Betty Crocker, and no one had heard of Martha Stewart.

When presented with the opportunity to write a book on vintage cakes a few years later, I returned to the treasure trove in the attic and started sifting through old recipes. I borrowed dog-eared cookbooks from family and friends and polled everyone about the cakes they remembered most from their childhoods. Word soon got out about the book, and I started receiving unsolicited recipes (accompanied by lovingly handwritten descriptions of their history) from all over. Everyone was passionate about a cake in their past!

I began to bake and rebake cakes (sometimes as many as six in one day), tinkering with the ingredients to revive and update vintage cake recipes for today's palate. Having tried the original recipes, I can attest that cakes used to be much sweeter than they are today. I cut down on the sugar and upped the flavors in my revised recipes. I also tested and retested a recipe until I found the right amounts of butter (for flavor) and oil (for moisture). My tinkering always included using wholesome, pure ingredients like nuts, oats, fruit, and chocolate in lieu of any inferior ingredients. And since we have so many more high-quality ingredients at our fingertips than cake bakers did a century ago, I had the luxury of being able to update vintage recipes by improving upon the raw materials in the ingredient list.

Every so often, I had the added challenge of attempting to reverse technology: what started in the early twentieth century as a delicious cake made from scratch often became a cake made with a cake mix beginning in the late 1940s. When cake mixes gained popularity, the scratch recipe was sometimes discarded (and lost) in favor of the more efficient—but never tastier—cake mix. In this book, I "deconstructed" a few cake mix classics (like Cherry Chip Cake, page 133, or Watergate Cake, page 99) to recapture the homemade recipe.

I've tried to include recipes for everyone's palate, from dense dark chocolate to light and airy chiffon to boozy Bundt cake, among others. And in gratitude for the bakery that left me all those vintage recipe cards, I've also included a slightly revised recipe for Champagne Cake (page 125), which can, of course, be tinted pink. It's my hope that you enjoy these vintage cakes, and that you find here some heirloom desserts to pass down to future generations.

THE CAKE BAKER'S BATTERY

You can't go wrong baking a cake if you stock your kitchen with the following equipment:

- An electronic baking scale (weighing the ingredients gives you a more accurate measurement than going by volume)
- A stand mixer (a high-powered handheld mixer will work, too, in a pinch)
- Rubber spatulas, wire whisks, and wooden spoons of all shapes and sizes
- A heatproof silicone spatula when cooking caramel or other high-heat concoctions
- Small and long thin metal spatulas (to spread fillings and frost cakes)
- Lots of mixing bowls, all sizes
- Measuring spoons and both dry and wet measuring cups
- A Microplane or other grater
- Metal strainers (fine mesh and medium mesh; they double as sifters)
- Cake pans: three 8 by 2-inch or two 9 by 2-inch round cake pans with straight sides, preferably aluminum; an 8 by 3-inch springform pan; a 9 by 13-inch baking dish; 10- and 12-cup metal tube pans; an angel food cake pan with feet; standard-size (1/3 cup) cupcake tins; and a 2 1/2-quart (9 by 9 by 2 1/2-inch) baking dish
- A cast-iron skillet
- Sauté pans and saucepans

- Biscuit cutters
- A rolling pin
- A timer (there's nothing like an overdone cake to remind you how important this tool can be . . .)
- Thermometers (one oven thermometer to ensure accuracy and one candy thermometer for heat-sensitive recipes)
- Parchment paper and baking spray
- Wooden skewers to test the cake in the oven or poke holes in the cake to allow the glaze to seep in
- A wire rack for cooling baked cakes
- A long thin slicing knife to halve a cake, and a good chef's knife to chop nuts and dried fruit, and so on
- Pastry brushes to coat cake layers with a sugar syrup
- A kitchen torch for browning meringue
- Piping bag and tips (or just a zip-top bag or two, if you aren't big on decorating)
- Cardboard rounds for moving and assembling cake layers (available at cake supply stores)
- A cake dome for storing cakes at room temperature
- A thick pair of oven mitts

THE CAKE BAKER'S CUPBOARD

The best piece of advice I can give anyone who wants to make a great cake is to start with the best ingredients. First-rate cake making is difficult to achieve with second-rate ingredients. The items to splurge on depend on the heart of the recipe: for a chocolate cake, it's high-quality chocolate or cocoa; for a custard, it's fresh farm eggs; for buttercream frosting, it's high-fat unsalted butter; and in all baking, it's always pure vanilla extract (the real thing). Here is a list of the ingredients I have on hand at all times, in case I want to whip up a cake on a moment's notice:

Almond Paste

This is a blend of finely ground blanched almonds and sugar, not to be confused with its sweeter, softer sibling, marzipan. Marzipan is strictly used for decorating, while almond paste is for suited for baking. My favorite brand of almond paste is Mandelin, which is a bit hard to come by, but the Internet can help you find it.

Brown Sugar

Choose cane over beet for its clean flavor and preferred baking traits. For a deeper taste, look for the less refined muscovado sugar, also known as Barbados sugar (especially when making the Maple Pecan Chiffon Cake, page 63).

Chocolate

Dark, semisweet, milk, and white chocolate. It really doesn't matter if the chocolate is in block form or chips, so long as it's good quality.

Cocoa

Both premium Dutch-processed cocoa and natural cocoa. These are two different types of cocoa and sometimes in a recipe it is crucial to use one and not the other—for a full explanation , see the sidebar on page 35. My favorite brands are Valrhona, Green & Black's, Droste, and Dagoba.

Coconut Milk

Not to be confused with cream of coconut (used in piña coladas) or coconut water (the liquid from the center of the coconut). Instead, coconut milk is the liquid exuded from the grated flesh of the coconut. It is most commonly found in cans in the ethnic foods aisle of your grocery. Be sure to select the full-fat variety. Always shake well before using and store any leftovers tightly covered in the refrigerator. It is quite perishable and will only last a few days after being opened.

Confectioners' Sugar

Also known as "powdered sugar" or "icing sugar," this is simply pulverized granulated sugar with a smidge of cornstarch added to prevent lumping. Use it mostly in frostings or sift it over finished cakes for added sweetness and a bit of decoration.

Dairy

Unsalted butter, large eggs, heavy cream (avoid ultrapasteurized if possible), whole milk, buttermilk, full-fat sour cream, plain full-fat yogurt, and mascarpone (found in the cheese section of the grocery store; my favorite brand is Galbani).

Dried Coconut

Read your recipe carefully so you get the right kind of coconut (sweetened or unsweetened; grated, shredded, flaked).

Dried Fruit

Select moist and plump dried fruit. If you wouldn't want to snack on it, you shouldn't try to bake with it!

Fine Sea Salt

Fine sea salt is now readily available in the grocery aisle. It has a clean taste and dissolves readily in baking recipes. Stay away from the iodized salt that our grandmothers grew up with (it has a chemical taste). I also avoid kosher salt in my baking—its coarse flakes don't sift well or dissolve easily in batters.

Flour

This is a key ingredient in most of the cakes in this book (with the exception of the Peppermint Patty Flourless Chocolate Cake, page 142). Use either an all-purpose flour or a cake flour. All-purpose flour is a blend of soft and hard wheat with a medium protein content of 9 to 12 percent, which allows it just the right strength and tenderness to be used in recipes from crusty breads to delicate cakes. Cake flour (often found in a box in the baking aisle) is milled from soft wheat, with a protein content of around 7 to 8 percent, and is often chlorinated (which makes it less acidic) and thus most commonly used in recipes where a tender, delicate crumb is desired. I always choose unbleached over bleached for any flour, when given the choice and occasionally like to throw whole wheat pastry flour into the mix for added texture and nutrients (try it in the Carrot Cake, page 94).

Fresh Fruit

Always try to source fruit that is in season and, preferably, local. Farmers' market vendors can help you pick out fruit that is at the peak of its season.

Granulated Sugar

Choose cane sugar over beet sugar (read the label!) for its better baking qualities—for example, cane sugar caramelizes better than beet sugar (especially important for the Old Vermont Burnt Sugar Cake, page 127, the Double Dip Caramel Cake, page 130, and any fruit upside-down cake).

Honey

Here's a great opportunity to support your local honey producers at farmers' markets or stores that source local foods. If by chance your honey crystallizes, bring it back to its natural state before incorporating it into your baking recipes:

place the container in a hot water bath until the honey becomes liquid again.

Leaveners

Baking soda, baking powder, and cream of tartar. Like spices, try to keep these fresh so they don't lose their oomph. Date the container upon purchase and discard it after a year.

Light Corn Syrup

Though it's hidden in the back corner of my cupboard, I always have a bottle of light corn syrup around for the occasional candy or frosting recipe. I am not a fan of GMO-based products (which most corn syrups are) and I haven't yet found an organic variety that I like. But as a syrup made from the starch of corn, it has many wondrous qualities. Its main use is to prevent sugar syrups from crystallizing, but it can also help pump up the volume in frostings and aid in maintaining soft textures in baked goods.

Liqueurs

Some of the recipes in this book call for specific liqueurs, others just offer suggestions. Let your taste buds be your guide.

Maple Syrup

My sweetener of choice; I use grade B syrup in my baking for its stronger flavor profile.

Molasses

A by-product of sugar production, molasses comes in three grades of refinement. Light molasses is less refined and slightly sweeter than the medium-refined dark variety. Blackstrap is the least sweet sort, and has a robust, bittersweet taste. I prefer the deep flavor of blackstrap in my baking. Whenever possible, choose unsulfured molasses.

Nuts

Store nuts in an airtight container in the freezer, where they will keep. Buy them from a busy store or at a farmers' market, where you know they will be fresh. See the sidebar for toasting nuts on page 114.

Other Grains

Rolled oats, oat flour, rice flour, and fine cornmeal.

Spices

My pantry includes ground cinnamon, whole cardamom, whole nutmeg, ground ginger, and whole cloves. To ensure that spices are fresh, purchase them either in small quantities or in the whole (not ground) form, and buy them in busy stores where there is a high turnover on the shelf. I use a handheld spice grater for my nutmeg and a clean electric coffee grinder for my cardamom and cloves.

Vanilla

Both pure vanilla extract and vanilla beans. My favorite vanilla comes from Madagascar.

TIPS AND TECHNIQUES

The best bakers I know pay attention to the details and use all their senses when they are in the kitchen. Here are some tricks of the trade that will help you make a great cake:

At the Batter Stage

- Review the list of ingredients and be sure you have everything you need. Don't substitute key ingredients or swap low-fat dairy for full-fat dairy (just promise yourself you will take a walk after the first slice of cake!).

- Read through the recipe once to be sure you understand each step. It's so disappointing to get halfway through a recipe and realize you accidentally added all the sugar when you were supposed to only add half a cup, or to see that the frosting that you haven't made yet needs to cool before you can frost the cake.

- Most recipes call for ingredients to be at room temperature, which is around 65° to 70°F. Try to set out any refrigerated ingredient that needs to be at room temperature about two hours before making the recipe. If time is limited, here are a few tips to speed up the process:

  ~ Uncracked eggs can be submerged in warm water for 5 minutes.

  ~ Measure dairy products into measuring cups and set the cups in bowls of warm water.

  ~ Cut butter into small cubes and separate the pieces.

- Prepare your pans and have them ready to go before you have finished mixing your batter. To prepare a cake pan, first spray or wipe your pan with canola oil or baking spray. If the recipe calls for lining the bottom of the pan with parchment paper, use the bottom of your pan as a guide to trace a circle on a piece of parchment paper, then cut out a circle just a smidge smaller than the traced circle. It should fit perfectly in the bottom of the pan without riding up the sides.

- Measure ingredients by weight if a weight is indicated. It's a more precise way to measure the ingredients, and is actually less effort.

- Measure liquid ingredients in a glass or plastic measuring cup on a flat surface; bend down to view the level of liquid in the cup to confirm the accuracy of your measurement.

- When measuring sticky ingredients like honey or peanut butter, spray a measuring cup with cooking spray first, and your ingredients will slide right out.

- If you are measuring dry ingredients by volume rather than weight, use cups with straight rims so the ingredients can be leveled off. Use the "fluff, scoop, and sweep" method to measure any dry ingredient: first fluff up the ingredient a bit (especially if it's flour), then scoop it up so that it overflows the measuring cup. Use a straight edge (like the back of a knife) to sweep off the excess.

- Always sift any lumpy ingredients (especially cocoa, cake flour, confectioners' sugar, oat flour, and cornstarch) before measuring. If the recipe calls for "1 cup of sifted cake flour," this means you should sift the flour *before* measuring it.

- When combining dry ingredients, sift AND whisk them. Why? Sifting only aerates the dry ingredients so they can be mixed into the batter with ease. Whisking ensures that the leavening agents and the salt are equally distributed throughout the batter, creating an even rise to the cake.

- Creaming, blending, whipping, folding: these are different terms that yield different results. Follow the mixing speed indicated in the recipe and always pay more attention to the visual cues than the times indicated in the recipes, since mixers vary.

  ~ *Creaming* is blending two ingredients together (like butter and sugar) to incorporate air and create an even mixture. The air trapped within the mixture will ultimately lead to the success of the cake by creating pockets where the leavening agents will do their magic and create a light cake. Creaming is best achieved with a stand mixer on medium-high to high speed. It is important that your butter is at room temperature (65° to 70°F), as butter that is too warm will render your cake greasy and dense, and butter that is too cold will lead to poor aeration. A properly creamed mixture will be light and fluffy and, if you're using butter, it will turn white.

  ~ *Blending* is combining ingredients until one disappears into the other. This is best done on low speed or by hand.

  ~ *Whipping* is what you do to cream or egg whites using a hand whisk or stand mixer with the whisk attachment. Begin slowly and increase the speed gradually as the contents of the bowl begin to thicken, taking care to avoid splashing the ingredients outside of the bowl.

  ~ *Folding* is the technique of gently blending one part of the batter into another while keeping as much volume as possible—which necessitates handling the batter as little as possible. Use a sturdy rubber spatula, a light hand, and a large bowl for this technique. Begin by distributing the lighter batter (usually whipped egg whites or cream) atop the heavier batter. Take your rubber spatula and picture the bowl as a clock: cut the spatula down through the middle of the batter from 12 o'clock to 6 o'clock, then turn your wrist to swoop the batter lightly up from the bottom of the bowl onto the top of the batter as you move the spatula from the bottom of the bowl to the side of the bowl at

9 o'clock and then out, turning your wrist and rolling the spatula over as you move to 3 o'clock, bringing the batter with you. (You can also think of this as drawing a cursive "J" in the batter.) Turn the bowl 90 degrees and repeat the same motion to gently and smoothly incorporate the lighter and heavier mixtures. Continue rotating the bowl and folding the mixture until it is just combined throughout and no pockets of heavy batter or light batter remain.

• Scrape the bowl as you go. Stop the mixer, grab a rubber spatula, and scrape down the sides and the bottom of the bowl and the paddle or utensil so no ingredients are sidelined while you mix the batter.

• Stop mixing the batter right after the ingredients have been incorporated. It's always best to finish the batter by hand so you don't accidentally overbeat it. Use a rubber spatula to scrape the sides and the bottom of the bowl and mix the ingredients until they are just unified.

• If a recipe calls for the batter to be divided into more than one cake pan, try to allocate the batter evenly between the pans to ensure that you make same-size cakes that bake in the same amount of time. You'll be most accurate if you use a scale (tare the pan first—that is, zero the weight of the pan so you don't accidentally include it in your measurement). If you don't have a scale, carefully eyeball your cake pans as you pour the batter into them.

At the Baking Stage

• Use the right size pan, or be prepared to adjust the baking time accordingly. If the recipe calls for an 8 by 2-inch round cake pan and you only have a 9 by 2-inch round cake pan, that's fine—just know that your cake will be thinner and will bake a few minutes faster than the time given in the recipe. If the recipe calls for an 8-inch round pan and you use an 8-inch square pan, again the cake will be thinner and bake faster. Generally, the contents of a 9-inch round pan fit perfectly in an 8-inch square pan and bake at the same rate.

• Be sure your oven is the right temperature. I recommend tucking a thermometer in the oven so you get an accurate read on how hot it is in there—many ovens run hotter or cooler than the temperature on the dial indicates.

• Bake the cake in the middle of the preheated oven, unless the recipe states otherwise. If your oven has hot spots, be sure to gently move the pans around halfway through baking time for even baking. Some ovens are smaller than others and might not be able to fit three pans on the same rack. If so, simply adjust two racks roughly in the middle and stagger your pans between the two, trying not to have pans directly above or below each other. Some oven racks are not level and the cakes turn out lopsided; if that's the case, build your layer cake by flipping one cake upside down so that when stacked, you have a level cake (your filling layers will be uneven, but this rarely matters).

- Check the cake at least 5 minutes before the time stated in the recipe. The baking times are guidelines. Rely instead on the visual cues for doneness that are described in the recipe. As a general rule, if the cake is pulling away from the sides, it is overdone. (A cake should only start to shrink from the sides after it has come out of the oven.) If it looks sunk, it needs more time. A cake will continue to bake a bit after it comes out of the oven.

- If you overbake a cake, it will be dry and have diminished flavor. If you are ever in this unfortunate position, a trick to revive an over-baked cake is to paint the layers with sugar syrup (see page 122).

- Almost always, cakes should cool off to room temperature before you do anything with them. Once cool, a cake can be wrapped airtight in plastic wrap and frozen—usually up to two months—until you want to frost and serve it. Assemble the cake with the layers still frozen, and allow the cake extra time to come to room temperature after it's been frosted. If you are delaying the assembly by only a day or two after baking, don't refrigerate the cake before you frost it; it's fine to keep it at room temperature wrapped air-tight.

At the Frosting Stage

Frosting the cake can be the *coup de grâce* or the *coup de désastre*. Here are some tricks of the trade:

- If the cake has domed in the middle and you intend to make a layer cake, you should cut off the domed part for all but the top layer. To do this, use a long serrated knife (it's helpful if it's longer than the cake is wide): place one hand on top of the layer to steady it and, holding the knife horizontally in your other hand, slowly cut off the domed part with a steady sawing motion.

- Pop your cake into the freezer for 15 minutes before you attempt to halve, assemble, or frost the cake; this step will make the cake firm and easier to work with.

- Some recipes call for you to cut a layer of cake into two or more thinner layers. Let your cake cool completely before you attempt to halve the layers (even better, freeze it for 15 minutes to firm it up). Place the cake on a flat surface. Take a long, thin slicing knife (a serrated or scalloped edge is preferable) and mark a line around the cake where you want to eventually cut (to halve the layer, the mark should be in the middle of the cake; if you are cutting a layer in thirds, work from the top to the bottom). After you have traced a line, rest the hand that isn't holding the knife on top of the cake to steady it. Slowly and confidently begin to saw into your cake, constantly checking that your knife is level and that you are following your line. Once you have cut all the way through the cake,

carefully separate the thin layers and cover them with plastic wrap to prevent them from drying out. Cardboard rounds can be helpful to move the fragile cake layers.

- Always bring your frosting to room temperature before you attempt to frost a cake, unless otherwise noted in the recipe.

- To keep your cake plate clean, slide a few strips of parchment paper or wax paper under the edges of the cake before you start to frost it. After you finish and the cake has set up, remove the paper.

- Moving the cake layers into position can be tricky business if you try to do it using only your hands. Instead, move the cake layer using a cardboard round or a flat metal disk (like the removable bottom of a tart pan).

- "Crumb coat" your cake by spreading a thin layer of frosting over it. You should be able to see the cake through the frosting. This step glues down the cake crumbs and gives your frosting a smoother surface to adhere to. After the crumb coating, place the cake in the refrigerator for 20 minutes to firm up before proceeding with the rest of the frosting. Once the crumb-coated cake has set up, remove it from the refrigerator. Using a thin metal spatula, spread a layer of the frosting on the sides of the cake, allowing the frosting to ride up the side, past the top layer. Spread the frosting on the sides thick enough to hide the cake underneath. Once you have frosted the sides, use your spatula to brush the frosting that is riding up the side over the top layer toward the center of the top of the cake, creating

a 90-degree angle between the sides and the top of the cake. Spread the top of the cake with any remaining frosting. Try not to lift up your spatula too quickly as you spread the frosting on the cake, or you might take some cake with you. You can use your spatula to swoop and swirl the frosting. For a more professional look, heat your spatula first under hot running water and smooth the sides and top of the frosted cake.

- To dress up a cake for a festive occasion, try any of these decorations:

  ~ **Piping:** While I tend to steer clear of fussy decorations, on occasion a little piping can be just the thing to finish a cake—the Black & White Cake (page 123), for example, just begs for chocolate kisses around the top edge of the cake. Instead of messing around with piping tubes with metal tips, I simply plop a spoonful or two of frosting into the bottom of a zip-top bag, seal it with as little air as possible, snip off one of the bottom corners, and squeeze the frosting out the hole. When I am done, I just throw the bag away. Easy! Equally handy are disposable piping bags, which you can buy at a cake decorating shop.

  ~ **Chocolate shavings:** A simple chocolate cake can look like a masterpiece if you shave some chocolate curls on the top. Use a sharp vegetable peeler to scrape curls from a slightly warm bar of chocolate.

  ~ **Confectioners' sugar:** To jazz up almost any cake, spoon confectioners' sugar into a fine-meshed sieve and tap the sieve gently over the top of the cake. Try it on the Blitz Torte (page 113) or Italian Cream Cake (page 105).

Or chill your cake so the frosting is firm, then lay a stencil or doily on top of the cake and use a fine-meshed sieve to lightly dust the top of the cake with confectioners' sugar. Carefully lift off the stencil or doily.

~ **Fresh fruit:** A handful of berries can make any cake sparkle.

~ **Fresh flowers:** Fresh cut flowers can change the look of a cake from innocent and sweet (violets) to formal and elegant (roses) to charming (pansies), or just add some punch (nasturtiums). Be sure to use clean, unsprayed flowers, and try to decorate your cake shortly before serving it so the blossoms don't look tired. Always use edible flowers; you never know when a guest will eat the decorations!

~ **Writing:** I prefer cakes without writing on them, as it is so easy to ruin a perfectly beautiful cake if you make a mistake! That said, if you want to write on your cake, here's the best way to do it: first, plan ahead how much space you need (writing out your message on a piece of scratch paper is helpful). Consider practicing on parchment paper before you attempt lettering on the cake itself. When you are ready to commit, start with the middle of your message and work from the middle of the cake out to the edge. For HAPPY BIRTHDAY, for example, start with the "BI" in the middle of the cake and work your way to the left and to the right. When you write, hold your elbow tucked in and your arm still. Move your entire upper body, not just your hand—as if you are swaying with your bag of frosting.

At the Storage Stage (if you get there)

Air is the enemy of cake! To prevent your cake from drying out, be sure to wrap it properly before storing.

• Only refrigerate a cake if it has a perishable filling or frosting (like whipped cream or cream cheese frosting). Bring the cake back to room temperature before serving; depending on the temperature of the room, this could take between 30 and 90 minutes.

• Any cake stored in the refrigerator should be wrapped airtight to prevent it from absorbing any odors lurking within. To keep from ruining a beautiful frosting job, for a cake covered in buttercream or cream cheese frosting, pop it in the refrigerator unwrapped until the frosting hardens, and then cover it with plastic wrap. For a soft cream–frosted cake, stick toothpicks into the cake's top and sides before draping plastic wrap over the toothpicks (the holes can easily be disguised before you serve the cake).

• For cakes stored at room temperature, cover the cake with a cake dome or other airtight barrier. Frosting protects a cake from drying out. Place a piece of plastic wrap over the cut part of the cake to keep the exposed part from drying out the cake.

Hasty Cakes

Here's a go-to set of recipes for when time is short but delicious cake is a must. There are no elaborate layers of buttercream or fussy techniques here to slow you down; instead, you'll find quick cakes, many of which don't even need a mixer or more than one bowl to make. From start to finish, most of these recipes can be made in an hour or so, including bake time. Just a drizzle of heavy cream over the top and you're ready to serve!

These recipes span our country's past, from colonial times when molasses-sweetened desserts were common (Shoo-Fly Cake, page 19) and cakes were typically baked in a cast-iron skillet (Blueberry Cornmeal Skillet Cake, page 25) up to the 1940s, when Ozark Pudding Cake (page 26) was served in the White House and desserts like Wacky Cake (page 21) and Berry Long Cake (page 17) were popular with frugal bakers for their inexpensive ingredients.

These are the pages in this book that will undoubtedly become splotched with butter stains and dotted with chocolate fingerprints from repeated use. For a crowd, try the super moist chocolate Texas Sheet Cake (page 22), loved by kids of all ages. If you want a cake you can pop out of the oven and onto the table, turn to the pear-studded Ozark Pudding Cake (page 26), which wafts heavenly aromas from an ironclad skillet. And for a quick cake you can eat for breakfast, lunch, or after dinner, try Lazy Daisy Oatmeal Cake (page 24), with all its coconut goodness. All of the cakes in this chapter are quick and easy to make, and even easier to eat!

Berry Long Cake with Ginger Crumb

The recipe for Strawberry Long Cake first appeared in a Betty Crocker advertisement in The American Weekly *in April 1945, touted as "super for supper . . . luscious for lunch!" Today, I would even eat it for breakfast. I've updated the recipe by adding cornmeal, which gives a pleasing texture. The cake was called a "long" cake because the frugal amount of strawberries in the original recipe went a long way. Here, I've augmented the berries so the name may not be entirely appropriate anymore. Blueberries or blackberries—or both—are equally as delicious as strawberries, especially with the ginger crumb topping.*

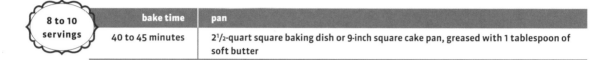

8 to 10 servings	bake time	pan
	40 to 45 minutes	2¹/₂-quart square baking dish or 9-inch square cake pan, greased with 1 tablespoon of soft butter

1 pound berries, left whole if small, sliced if larger (6 cups prepped)

¹/₂ cup (3¹/₂ ounces) sugar

2 tablespoons brandy or pure vanilla extract

TOPPING

¹/₃ cup (2¹/₂ ounces) firmly packed brown sugar

¹/₄ cup (1¹/₄ ounces) all-purpose flour

¹/₄ cup (1¹/₂ ounces) diced candied ginger

4 tablespoons (2 ounces) unsalted butter, at room temperature, cut into small cubes

CAKE

1¹/₂ cups (7¹/₂ ounces) all-purpose flour

¹/₂ cup (2³/₄ ounces) fine cornmeal

¹/₂ cup (3¹/₂ ounces) sugar

2 teaspoons baking powder

1 teaspoon ground ginger

1 teaspoon fine sea salt

6 tablespoons (3 ounces) unsalted butter, cut into small cubes

2 eggs

²/₃ cup whole milk

Center an oven rack and preheat the oven to 375°F.

In a large bowl, toss together the berries with the sugar and the brandy or vanilla. Set aside at room temperature while making the rest of the cake.

To make the topping, combine the sugar, flour, and ginger in a small bowl. Blend the butter into the dry ingredients, using either your fingertips or a fork, until the mixture forms crumbs. Put the topping in the freezer while you mix the cake batter.

To make the cake, combine the flour, cornmeal, sugar, baking powder, ginger, and salt in a large bowl. Add the butter and using your fingertips, work it completely into the dry ingredients. In a separate bowl, whisk the eggs and milk together and stir them into the dry ingredients until combined. Spread the batter into your buttered pan. Evenly distribute the sugared berries on top of the batter. Scatter the chilled topping over the berries. Place the dish in the center of the oven. Bake until the berries bubble and the cake is firm (ignoring those places where the crumb topping has melted into the cake, since it's hard to tell in those oh-so-buttery spots), 40 to 45 minutes.

Cool the cake on a wire rack for 30 minutes and serve warm from the dish.

Well wrapped and stored at room temperature, this cake keeps for up to 2 days.

Rhubarb Pudding Cake

Fresh rhubarb is at its peak in spring, and this casual comfort food cake makes the most of it. The "pudding" in the cake is created by pouring a hot, vanilla-infused rhubarb compote over a thick sour cream batter. I found the idea for the cake in my mother's copy of the Farm Journal's Country Cookbook, *first published in 1959. I've jazzed it up a bit with the addition of vanilla and the richness of sour cream (feel free to substitute full-fat plain yogurt). This dessert's as fitting scooped out of the pan and into a bowl for breakfast as it is served with ice cream for dessert.*

8 to 10 servings	bake time	pan
	45 to 50 minutes	2¹/₂-quart square baking dish or 9-inch square cake pan, greased with 1 tablespoon of soft butter

1 pound rhubarb, trimmed of leaves and ends, diced (4 cups)

1¹/₂ cups (10¹/₂ ounces) sugar

¹/₄ vanilla bean, split lengthwise

¹/₂ cup water

1²/₃ cups (8¹/₃ ounces) all-purpose flour

1¹/₂ teaspoons baking powder

¹/₂ teaspoon fine sea salt

¹/₂ cup (4 ounces) unsalted butter, at room temperature

2 eggs

2 teaspoons pure vanilla extract

1 cup (9 ounces) full-fat sour cream or whole milk yogurt, at room temperature

Ice cream, for serving (optional)

Center an oven rack and preheat the oven to 350°F.

Make a compote by tossing together the rhubarb and 1 cup of the sugar in a medium heavy saucepan with a lid. Add the vanilla bean and water, cover, and simmer over medium heat for about 10 minutes, until the rhubarb is soft but has not completely broken down. Give the rhubarb a stir or two while it is cooking. Take the compote off the heat but keep it covered so it will stay warm while you make the cake.

To make the cake, sift together the flour, baking powder, and salt in a bowl, then whisk the ingredients by hand to ensure they are well mixed.

In the bowl of a stand mixer with the paddle attachment, cream the butter and the remaining ¹/₂ cup of sugar together on medium-high speed until fluffy, about 5 minutes. As you make the batter, stop the mixer frequently and scrape the paddle and the sides of the bowl with a rubber spatula. Blend in the eggs one at a time, adding the second egg as soon as the first one has disappeared into the batter, followed by the vanilla. Blend in the flour mixture in three parts, alternating with the sour cream in two parts, so that you begin and end with the flour mixture.

Spread the batter into the prepared dish or pan and distribute the compote over the top. The compote will be quite runny, but don't fear: all will be well once the cake has baked. Place the cake in the center of the oven and bake until the edges are firm and the center no longer jiggles, 45 to 50 minutes. Let the cake cool for about 30 minutes, then spoon it right from the pan into bowls and top with a scoop of ice cream.

This cake is best the day it is made, but well-wrapped it can be stored at room temperature for up to 2 days.

Shoo-Fly Cake

Here's a simple molasses spice cake that takes its lead from the old Pennsylvania Dutch favorite, shoo-fly pie. Although the origin of the name is up for debate, the settlers of southeastern Pennsylvania surely waved plenty of flies away from their sticky, sweet pie as it cooled, perhaps giving rise to its name. Topped with crumb, this cake is as good for breakfast as it is for dessert served with a scoop of chocolate ice cream. This recipe hails from my Great Grandma Burkholder's recipe collection, and she was born in 1895. Now that's vintage!

8 to 10 servings	bake time	pan
	45 minutes	9 by 2-inch round cake pan, greased with 1 tablespoon of soft butter

CRUMB TOPPING

1/3 cup (2 1/2 ounces) firmly packed brown sugar

3/4 cup (3 3/4 ounces) all-purpose flour

1/4 cup (2 ounces) unsalted butter, at room temperature, cut into small cubes

CAKE

1 cup (7 ounces) sugar

3/4 cup (6 ounces) unsalted butter, melted

3/4 cup (9 ounces) unsulfured blackstrap molasses

2 teaspoons pure vanilla extract

2 eggs

2 1/2 cups (12 1/2 ounces) all-purpose flour

2 teaspoons ground ginger

1 teaspoon ground cinnamon

1 teaspoon baking soda

1/2 teaspoon fine sea salt

1 cup warm coffee (can be reheated from the morning brew)

Center an oven rack and preheat the oven to 350°F.

To make the crumb topping, combine the brown sugar and the flour in a small bowl. Toss in the butter cubes and, using your fingertips, pinch the butter into the dry ingredients to form crumbs. Place the bowl in the freezer while you make the cake.

To make the cake, whisk together the sugar, butter, molasses, and vanilla in a large bowl until smooth. Blend in the eggs one at a time.

In a separate bowl, sift together the flour, ginger, cinnamon, baking soda, and salt, then whisk the ingredients by hand to ensure they are well mixed. Using a rubber spatula, stir the flour mixture into the batter in three additions, alternating with the coffee in two additions, beginning and ending with the flour mixture. Pour the thin batter into the prepared pan and sprinkle with the chilled crumb topping. Bake in the center of the oven until the top is firm, about 45 minutes. Cool the cake on a wire rack for about 30 minutes before serving warm from the pan.

Well wrapped and kept at room temperature, this cake keeps for 3 days.

A Molasses Moment

Molasses is a thick dark syrup. The British call it treacle, which is a generic term for any syrup made as a by-product of refining sugar cane. Molasses was a popular and economical substitute for refined white sugar in the eighteenth century. By the end of the nineteenth century, it competed with maple sugar and white refined sugar as America's chosen sweetener. When sugar prices dropped after World War I, molasses and maple sugar both fell in popularity. Today, molasses is used when its rich and tangy taste is sought after—as it is for shoo-fly pie!

Grammy Cake

This simple chocolate tube cake was the cake of my father's childhood, and in turn became the cake of my youth. My paternal grandmother got the recipe in 1949 from her next-door neighbor, Marge Mentes. My Grammy used to ship it (unglazed) to my father and his brothers when they were in college and in the military. At some point, the cake was dubbed "Grammy Cake," and the name stuck. As generations of Richardsons can attest, this cake is sturdy, reliable, and delicious. Use a good natural cocoa (Scharffen Berger and Dagoba both come to mind) and if you aren't shipping the cake, glaze it with chocolate ganache for a decadent treat.

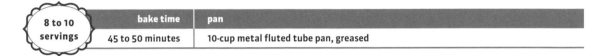

8 to 10 servings	bake time	pan
	45 to 50 minutes	10-cup metal fluted tube pan, greased

½ cup (1¾ ounces) lightly packed premium unsweetened natural cocoa (see Cocoa Confusion, page 35)

1 teaspoon baking soda

1 cup boiling water

¾ cup (6 ounces) unsalted butter, cut into small cubes

¼ cup canola oil

2 cups (10 ounces) all-purpose flour

1½ cups (10½ ounces) granulated sugar

½ cup (3¾ ounces) firmly packed brown sugar

½ teaspoon fine sea salt

3 eggs

1 tablespoon pure vanilla extract

Confectioners' sugar, for dusting, or ¾ cup Chocolate Ganache (page 146), for glazing

Center an oven rack and preheat the oven to 350°F.

Whisk together the cocoa and baking soda in a bowl. Whisk in the boiling water; the mixture will bubble. Add the butter cubes and oil and whisk occasionally to melt the butter. Set aside to cool to room temperature.

Sift together the flour, sugars, and salt in a large bowl, then whisk the ingredients by hand to ensure they are well mixed.

Add the eggs and vanilla to the cocoa mixture and whisk to combine. Slowly pour the cocoa mixture into the dry ingredients while stirring with a rubber spatula; stop stirring once the mixture has just combined and is free of lumps. Pour the mixture into the prepared tube pan and place in the center of the oven until a wooden skewer inserted in the middle comes out with moist crumbs attached, 45 to 50 minutes.

Cool the cake in its pan on a wire rack for 30 minutes before inverting it onto a serving plate. Grammy Cake tastes great when still warm with a light dusting of confectioners' sugar sifted through a fine mesh sieve. For a fancier version, pour warm chocolate ganache over the cooled cake.

This cake is a good keeper (and shipper!) when well wrapped and kept at room temperature. It should last up to 5 days.

Wacky Cake

Wacky Cake, Crazy Cake, Puddle Cake: whatever you want to call it, this cake is a snap to make. You can find a recipe for this cake in every church and Junior League cookbook for the past century under various names that reflect the ingredients and method of making it. Straight into the cake pan—not a mixing bowl—you pour each wet ingredient (oil, water, and vinegar) into a separate well in the dry ingredients, creating puddles, before you mix and bake the cake. Talk about wacky! I was always leery of making this recipe since the ingredients sounded like a turn-off (no eggs, no butter?!)—but boy, was I wrong! Here, I do veer off the original method, which I must admit is a bit too wacky for me.

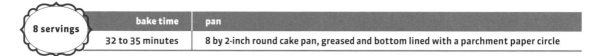

8 servings	bake time	pan
	32 to 35 minutes	8 by 2-inch round cake pan, greased and bottom lined with a parchment paper circle

1½ cups (7½ ounces) all-purpose flour

1 cup (7 ounces) sugar

6 tablespoons (1⅓ ounce) lightly packed premium unsweetened natural cocoa (see Cocoa Confusion, page 35)

1 teaspoon baking soda

½ teaspoon fine sea salt

1 cup cold water

⅓ cup canola oil

1 tablespoon white vinegar

1 teaspoon pure vanilla extract

Confectioners' sugar for dusting, or ¾ cup Chocolate Ganache (page 146), for frosting

Center an oven rack and preheat the oven to 350°F.

In a large bowl, sift together the flour, sugar, cocoa, baking soda, and salt, then whisk the ingredients by hand to ensure they are well mixed.

In a separate bowl, whisk together the water, oil, vinegar, and vanilla.

Pour the wet ingredients into the dry ingredients and stir until just combined. Dump the batter into the prepared pan and spread it into an even layer. Place in the middle of the oven and bake until a skewer inserted in the middle comes out with moist crumbs attached, 32 to 35 minutes.

Cool the cake on a wire rack for 30 minutes before inverting and removing the pan. Wacky cake tastes great when still warm. Serve it with a light dusting of powdered sugar or glazed with warm chocolate ganache.

Well wrapped and stored at room temperature, this cake keeps for up to 3 days.

Texas Sheet Cake

When time is tight and you need to throw something together for a picnic or a potluck or a bake sale, this is the perfect crowd pleaser. It's a large, thin layer of tender chocolate cake slathered with gooey chocolate frosting and sprinkled with toasted nuts. The frosting gets poured onto the cake when they are both still warm. Some say "don't mess with Texas," but this cake can easily be spiced up by adding a teaspoon of cinnamon to the dry ingredients or by swapping coffee for the hot water.

Serves a crowd	bake time	pan
	32 to 35 minutes	15 by 10 by 2-inch baking pan, greased

CAKE

1 cup (8 ounces) unsalted butter

1/2 cup (1³/4 ounces) lightly packed premium unsweetened natural cocoa (see Cocoa Confusion, page 35)

3 tablespoons canola oil

1 cup water

2 cups (10 ounces) all-purpose flour

2 cups (14 ounces) sugar

1 teaspoon baking soda

1/2 teaspoon fine sea salt

2 eggs

1/2 cup buttermilk

2 teaspoons pure vanilla extract

FROSTING

1/2 cup (4 ounces) unsalted butter

1/4 cup (1 ounce) lightly packed premium unsweetened cocoa, preferably Dutch-processed

1/3 cup whole milk

2 teaspoons pure vanilla extract

3 cups (12 ounces) sifted confectioners' sugar

1/2 cup (2¹/8 ounces) toasted chopped nuts (such as walnuts, pecans, or hazelnuts; see Toasting Nuts, page 114)

Center an oven rack and preheat the oven to 375°F.

To make the cake, melt the butter in a large saucepan over medium heat. Whisk in the cocoa. Add the oil and water and bring to a rolling boil for 30 seconds. Remove the pan from the heat and set it aside to cool slightly. Meanwhile, sift together the flour, sugar, baking soda, and salt in a large bowl, then whisk the ingredients by hand to ensure they are well mixed. Pour the warm cocoa mixture into the sifted ingredients and whisk until just combined. In a small bowl, whisk together the eggs, buttermilk, and vanilla. With a rubber spatula, stir the buttermilk mixture into the batter. Pour the batter into the greased pan and place in the center of the oven. Bake until the top is firm and a wooden skewer inserted in the middle of the cake comes out with moist crumbs, 32 to 35 minutes.

While the cake is in the oven, make the frosting: melt the butter in a saucepan over medium heat. Whisk in the cocoa and bring the mixture to a rolling boil; boil for 30 seconds. Remove from heat and whisk in the milk and vanilla. Add the confectioners' sugar 1 cup at a time while whisking continuously. Immediately after the cake comes out of the oven, pour the frosting over the hot cake and sprinkle with the nuts. Try not to jiggle the cake before it sets or you'll leave waves in the frosting. Allow to cool before cutting into squares.

Well wrapped and stored at room temperature, this cake keeps for up to 5 days.

Lazy Daisy Oatmeal Cake

My mother-in-law, Betty Kappler, gave me the recipe for Lazy Daisy Oatmeal Cake. I modified it by adding coconut milk, which adds a touch of richness to the otherwise uncomplicated batter. It's quick to make and oh-so-versatile; I enjoy it as dessert, at brunch, or just with a cup of coffee. Use old-fashioned rolled oats here, not quick-cooking or instant, and don't forget to shake the can of coconut milk well before opening it.

8 to 10 servings	bake time	pan
	35 to 40 minutes	9 by 2-inch round cake pan, greased and bottom lined with a parchment paper circle

CAKE

1 cup (3¹/₂ ounces) old-fashioned oats

¹/₂ cup (4 ounces) unsalted butter, cut into small cubes

¹/₂ cup coconut milk

1 cup boiling water

³/₄ cup (5¹/₄ ounces) granulated sugar

³/₄ cup (5²/₃ ounces) firmly packed brown sugar

2 eggs

2 teaspoons pure vanilla extract

1¹/₂ cups (7¹/₂ ounces) all-purpose flour

1 teaspoon baking soda

¹/₂ teaspoon ground cinnamon

¹/₂ teaspoon ground ginger

¹/₂ teaspoon fine sea salt

ICING

1 cup (4 ounces) lightly packed sweetened shredded, coconut

¹/₂ cup (3³/₄ ounces) firmly packed brown sugar

¹/₂ cup (2 ounces) pecans, chopped (see Toasting Nuts, page 114)

¹/₂ cup (1³/₄ ounces) old-fashioned oats

¹/₄ cup coconut milk

¹/₄ cup (2 ounces) unsalted butter, melted

Center an oven rack and preheat the oven to 350°F.

To make the cake, place the oats, butter, and coconut milk in the bowl of a stand mixer. Pour the boiling water over the oat mixture, cover with a lid or plastic wrap and let stand for 20 minutes.

Remove the lid and give the oats a good stir to combine the ingredients. Blend in the sugars, followed by the eggs and the vanilla. Using the paddle attachment, mix on medium-high until well beaten, about 2 minutes.

Sift the flour, soda, cinnamon, ginger, and salt together into a bowl, then whisk the ingredients by hand to ensure they are well mixed. Dump the flour mixture into the batter and mix on low speed until just combined. Scrape down the sides of the bowl well to ensure the ingredients are fully blended.

Pour the batter into the prepared pan, smooth the top, and place the pan in the center of the oven. Bake until a wooden skewer inserted in the middle comes out clean and the cake springs back when lightly touched, 35 to 40 minutes.

Cool the cake on a wire rack for 10 minutes while you make the icing.

To make the icing, combine the coconut, sugar, nuts, and oats in a small bowl. Stir in the coconut milk and melted butter until the mixture is blended.

Preheat the broiler. Pour the icing evenly over the cake, gently spreading it out to the edge of the pan. Place the cake in the middle of the oven under the broiler. Broil until the icing bubbles and turns golden brown, about 2 minutes, watching vigilantly to prevent the icing from burning.

Cool the cake on the wire rack for 30 minutes. Serve the cake warm, directly from the pan.

Well wrapped and stored at room temperature, this cake keeps for 3 days.

Blueberry Cornmeal Skillet Cake

Skillet cakes were common in colonial times, back when bakers went to the blacksmith for their baking wares. Cake pans were not common until later in the nineteenth and into the early twentieth century, once stainless steel and aluminum became more economical. I love baking desserts in my grandmother's Wagner cast-iron skillet and look for any opportunity to make a skillet cake. Here, the flavors of corn and blueberries complement each other. Not blueberry season? Try different seasonal fruit—sour cherries in late spring, huckleberries in fall, or cranberries in winter.

8 servings	bake time	pan
	48 to 50 minutes	10-inch cast-iron skillet

1¼ cups (6¼ ounces) all-purpose flour

1½ teaspoons baking powder

½ teaspoon fine sea salt

¼ teaspoon baking soda

¾ cup (4⅛ ounces) fine cornmeal

½ cup (4 ounces) unsalted butter

½ cup (6 ounces) honey

2 eggs, at room temperature

1 cup (9 ounces) full-fat yogurt or sour cream

10 ounces blueberries, fresh or frozen (2 cups)

¼ cup (1¾ ounces) firmly packed brown sugar

Ice cream, for serving (optional)

Center an oven rack and preheat the oven to 350°F.

Sift together the flour, baking powder, salt, and baking soda in a bowl. Add the cornmeal and whisk the ingredients by hand to ensure that they are well mixed. Set aside.

Melt the butter in the iron skillet you plan to use to bake the cake, swirling it to coat the bottom and sides of the pan. Pour the melted butter into a bowl and whisk in the honey, the eggs, and the yogurt or sour cream. Pour the liquid ingredients into the dry ingredients and stir until just barely combined. Fold in half of the blueberries. Dump the batter into the skillet and spread it into an even layer. Distribute the remainder of the blueberries evenly on top of the batter and sprinkle with brown sugar. Place the skillet in the middle of the oven and bake until a wooden skewer inserted in the middle comes out with moist crumbs attached, 48 to 50 minutes. (The heat from the pan will continue to bake the cake after it is removed from the oven, so take care to remove it when it is just barely done.) Serve warm from the skillet, either as-is for breakfast or with a scoop of ice cream for dessert.

This cake is best the day it is baked but keeps for up to 2 days if well wrapped and stored at room temperature.

Cast-Iron Skillets

Cast-iron skillets are great for baking because they distribute and retain heat well. In the late nineteenth century, cast-iron stoves were common in American kitchens and cast-iron skillets were a fixture on the hearth. Season these durable pans with a bit of vegetable oil to protect them from rusting, and you'll be able to pass down your own vintage cookware!

Ozark Pudding Cake

An apple cake from the Midwest, this humble dessert leapt in popularity when Bess Truman, President Harry Truman's wife, made Ozark pudding for guests of the White House. In 1946, she even put this dessert on the menu for a dinner with Winston Churchill. My spin on this old favorite is to substitute pears for the apples. If you use Bartlett pears, the skins are so thin you don't need to peel them.

8 servings	bake time	pan
	38 to 40 minutes	10-inch cast-iron skillet, greased with 1 tablespoon of soft butter

2 large ripe but firm pears, peeled, quartered, and cored

1 cup (5 ounces) all-purpose flour

1 teaspoon baking powder

1 teaspoon ground ginger

½ teaspoon fine sea salt

4 tablespoons (2 ounces) unsalted butter, at room temperature

1 cup (7 ounces) plus 1 teaspoon sugar

1 egg, at room temperature

1 teaspoon pure vanilla extract

½ cup (2 ounces) sliced natural almonds, toasted

½ cup (2¼ ounces) dried cranberries (optional)

Vanilla ice cream, for serving (optional)

Center an oven rack and preheat the oven to 350°F.

Finely chop one of the pears and thinly slice the other.

Sift together the flour, baking powder, ginger, and salt in a bowl, and then whisk the mixture by hand to ensure that the ingredients are well mixed.

Using a stand mixer fitted with the paddle attachment, blend the butter and sugar together on medium speed until the mixture resembles wet sand. Add the egg and vanilla and blend on medium-high speed until fluffy, about 5 minutes. Scrape down the bowl occasionally as needed. Turn the mixer to low speed and add the flour mixture all at once. Mix until just blended. The batter will be stiff.

Using a rubber spatula, fold in the chopped pear (setting aside the sliced pear for the top), half the almonds, and the cranberries, and stir just until blended. Dump the batter into the prepared skillet and spread it in an even layer. Arrange the pear slices on top of the batter and sprinkle with the remaining almonds and the remaining teaspoon of sugar. Place the skillet in the middle of the oven and bake until the cake is golden in color and the center springs back when lightly touched, 38 to 40 minutes. (The heat from the pan will continue to bake the cake after it is removed from the oven, so take care to remove it when it is just barely done.) Serve warm from the skillet with a scoop of vanilla ice cream.

This cake is best the day it is baked. Well covered, it keeps in the skillet for up to 2 days at room temperature.

Everyday Cakes

Cakes have come a long way from their origin as spiritual offerings to the gods of ancient civilizations. These days, cakes no longer take on religious meaning or even require a special occasion; they have evolved into an everyday affair due to the ready availability of ingredients and the ease of the modern American kitchen. This chapter is full of irresistible recipes to have at your fingertips when you just want to make a cake but have no particular event (or spiritual offering!) in mind.

It was tough pinning down the actual origins of a few of the cakes in this chapter; many of them either made their debut or hit their peak of popularity in the twentieth century. Icebox cakes, for example, gained popularity between 1930 and 1950, when refrigerators became a mainstream household appliance. The Honey Bee Cake (page 31) originated in 1954 in Cincinnati, Ohio, at a commercial bakery research department. Kentucky Bourbon Cake (page 45) dates back well before the 1960s but became popular in 1963 when it was a prize-winning cake at a Pillsbury Bake-Off competition in Missouri. And the Harvey Wallbanger cocktail was introduced in the 1950s before giving rise to the spiked cake of the same name (page 46) that became all the rage almost twenty years later.

Honey Bee Cake

This cake has such a folksy name, yet its origins are anything but! The recipe came from the Procter & Gamble Bakery Research Department, circa 1954. I love our regional blackberry honey and use it in many of my recipes, but let your taste dictate which variety of honey to use—acacia, clover, wildflower, fireweed, orange blossom, and tupelo honey are all great for baking. What matters is that you love the taste of the honey you choose, since that's the prevailing flavor in this cake. Feel free to substitute any variety of nuts—hazelnuts, pecans, walnuts, and pinenuts all come to mind—for the almonds in this recipe, or even try coconut (which I know is not a nut). I love to serve this cake while it's still a little warm, with a dollop of crème fraîche.

8 to 10 servings	bake time	pan
	45 to 50 minutes	9 by 2-inch round cake pan or 9 by 3-inch springform pan, greased and bottom lined with a parchment paper circle

CAKE

2¼ cups (11¼ ounces) all-purpose flour

2 teaspoons baking powder

1 teaspoon fine sea salt

¾ cup plus 2 tablespoons (7 ounces) unsalted butter, at room temperature

¾ cup (5¼ ounces) sugar

⅓ cup (4 ounces) honey

2 teaspoons pure vanilla extract

2 eggs, at room temperature

1 egg yolk, at room temperature

¾ cup buttermilk, at room temperature

GLAZE

½ cup (6 ounces) honey

¼ cup (1¾ ounces) firmly packed brown sugar

¼ cup (2 ounces) unsalted butter

Heaping ½ cup (2 ounces) natural sliced almonds, toasted (see Toasting Nuts, page 114)

Center an oven rack and preheat the oven to 350°F.

In a bowl, sift together the flour, baking powder, and salt, then whisk the ingredients by hand to ensure they are well mixed.

In the bowl of a stand mixer fitted with the paddle attachment, combine the butter, sugar, honey, and vanilla on low speed until blended; increase the speed to high and cream until very light and fluffy, 5 to 7 minutes. As you make the batter, stop the mixer frequently and scrape the paddle and the sides of the bowl with a rubber spatula. Blend in the eggs and egg yolk one at a time, adding the next one as soon as the previous one has disappeared into the batter. With the mixer on low speed, add the flour mixture in three parts, alternating with the buttermilk in two parts, beginning and ending with the flour. After each addition, mix until just barely blended and stop and scrape the bowl. Stop the mixer before the last of the flour has been incorporated and complete the blending by hand with a rubber spatula to ensure you do not overbeat the batter.

Spread the thick batter evenly into the prepared pan. Rap the pan firmly on the counter to release any air bubbles. Place the pan in the center of the oven and bake for 45 minutes. The cake will turn a deep golden color and be firm on top, and a wooden skewer inserted in the middle will have moist crumbs attached. The cake might crack on the surface as it bakes; don't worry, this simply provides a way for the cake to soak up more honey glaze.

continued

While the cake is in the oven, make the glaze in a small saucepan by stirring the honey, sugar, and butter over medium heat until combined. Bring the mixture just barely to a simmer. Turn off the heat but leave the saucepan on the burner to keep warm.

Remove the cake from the oven and poke holes all over the top of the cake with a wooden skewer. Pour half of the glaze over the cake, evenly sprinkle the cake with the almonds, and then pour the rest of the glaze over the almonds.

Place the pan back in the center of the oven and bake for an additional 5 minutes.

Cool the cake on a wire rack for about an hour. To remove the cake from the pan, turn the cake upside down onto a plate (not your serving plate), remove the pan and the parchment paper, then place your serving plate on the bottom of the cake and flip it back over. (If you use a springform pan, remove the sides of the pan before flipping the cake and removing the parchment paper.) Serve just barely warm.

The honey in this cake makes it a good keeper (5 days) when well wrapped and stored at room temperature.

Pearl's Chocolate Macaroon Cake

Here's a delicious chocolate ring cake with a chewy coconut macaroon layer baked inside. There are many vintage recipes for chocolate macaroon cake, and this one was lovingly passed down to me by a baker who got it from her grandmother Pearl. You will use at least four small bowls and two big bowls to make this recipe, but it's well worth the mess!

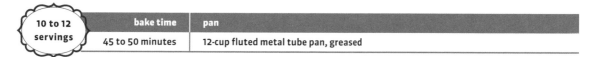

10 to 12 servings	bake time	pan
	45 to 50 minutes	12-cup fluted metal tube pan, greased

4 eggs, at room temperature

1 teaspoon fine sea salt

2 cups (14 ounces) sugar

1 tablespoon pure vanilla extract

2 cups (8 ounces) lightly packed sweetened shredded coconut

2 cups (10 ounces) plus 1 tablespoon all-purpose flour

$^{1}/_{2}$ cup (2 ounces) lightly packed premium Dutch-processed cocoa (see Cocoa Confusion, page 35)

$^{3}/_{4}$ cup hot brewed coffee

$^{1}/_{2}$ cup (4$^{1}/_{2}$ ounces) sour cream

2 teaspoons baking powder

$^{1}/_{2}$ cup (4 ounces) unsalted butter, at room temperature

2 tablespoons canola oil

$^{3}/_{4}$ cup Chocolate Ganache (page 146)

Center an oven rack and preheat the oven to 350°F.

Separate the eggs, placing the yolks in a small bowl and the whites in a mixing bowl. Using a stand mixer fitted with the whisk attachment, add $^{1}/_{2}$ teaspoon of the salt to the whites and combine at low speed. Gradually increase the speed to medium-high, whipping until the whites just form soft peaks. With the mixer running, slowly add $^{3}/_{4}$ cup of the sugar in a steady stream and continue whipping until the whites hold a firm peak. Transfer 1 cup (3$^{3}/_{4}$ ounces) of the mixture to a small bowl and fold in 1 teaspoon of the vanilla, all of the coconut, and 1 tablespoon of the flour to make the coconut filling. Set aside both the coconut filling and the remaining meringue mixture at room temperature.

In a small bowl, whisk together the cocoa, hot coffee, and sour cream. In a separate bowl, sift together the remaining 2 cups of flour with the baking powder and the remaining $^{1}/_{2}$ teaspoon of salt, and then whisk the dry ingredients by hand to ensure they are well blended.

In the clean bowl of a stand mixer fitted with the paddle attachment, mix the remaining 1$^{1}/_{4}$ cups of sugar with the butter, oil, and remaining 2 teaspoons of vanilla on low speed until blended; increase the speed to high for 5 minutes. Stop the mixer frequently and scrape the paddle and the sides of the bowl with a rubber spatula. Blend in the egg yolks, two at a time, adding the next two as soon as the previous two have disappeared into the batter. With the mixer on low speed, add the flour mixture in three parts, alternating with the cocoa mixture in two parts, beginning and ending with the flour. After each addition, mix until just barely blended and stop and scrape the bowl. Blend in the final addition of flour by hand

continued

with a rubber spatula to ensure you do not overbeat the batter. Fold in the remaining (noncoconut) meringue.

Spoon half the batter into the prepared pan (half will be approximately 1 pound 6 ounces) and spread it evenly to the sides. Drop spoonfuls of the coconut filling on top of the batter, trying your best to keep it away from the outside edge while creating a ring around the center of the cake. Spoon the remaining half of the batter on top of the filling and spread the batter evenly. Place the pan in the center of the oven and bake until a wooden skewer inserted in the middle comes out with moist crumbs attached, 45 to 50 minutes. Remove the cake to a rack and allow it to cool to room temperature before removing it from the pan. (I found out the hard way that this cake is very fragile when it is warm!) Once it's cool, remove the cake from the pan and place it on a serving plate. Glaze with warm chocolate ganache.

This cake is a great keeper (5 days) when kept in an airtight container at room temperature.

Cocoa Confusion

Cocoa powder falls into two categories: natural and Dutch-processed. Cocoa is naturally slightly acidic, a characteristic that can make it taste harsh or bitter. Dutch-processed cocoa is treated to remove some of its natural acidity; the result is a darker, mellowed cocoa flavor. Read the label: if it says "treated with alkaline" or "alkalized," this means it has been Dutch-processed.

Dutch-processed cocoa is commonly used for frostings; natural cocoa is more commonly found in recipes for baked products, since the baking process neutralizes the acids somewhat. The two types of cocoa are not interchangeable. Use the type that is called for in the recipe, lest a substitution alter the results. The cocoa called for in a recipe has been matched with the recipe's leavening ingredients to balance the recipe's acidity or alkalinity. If you substitute Dutch-processed for natural cocoa, the batter may lack acidity, in which case it will not set (picture a big flat cookie or a cake that is more akin to pudding). On the other hand, if you use natural cocoa in place of Dutch-processed cocoa, the batter may be too alkaline, in which case the cake may be overleavened and may sink in the middle as it cools.

Just as no two chocolate bars taste quite the same, so too with the different brands of cocoa powder. The chocolaty flavor varies tremendously. When shopping for cocoa powder, stay away from the bulk bins and search out cocoa made by chocolatiers; their cocoa powders will be of higher quality. My favorite retail brands are Valrhona, Green & Black's, Droste, and Dagoba. Once you find a brand you like (as I have with the Cacao Barry Extra Brute Cocoa we use at the bakery), stick with it.

To add to the complexity, cocoa butter content differs among various cocoa powders, varying from 10 percent to 35 percent. As a result, some cocoa powders are denser and their ratio of weight to volume will vary from other cocoa powders. For example, one ounce of cocoa powder may measure anywhere from 3 tablespoons to over $1/2$ cup! The recipes in this book were developed based on ingredient weight, so I recommend that, when in doubt, you use the weight measurement. If you are measuring by volume, sift any lumps out of the cocoa powder before you measure it, and then lightly pack the measuring cup.

Lemon and Almond Streamliner Cake

I found a recipe for a Lemon Stream Liner cake tucked away in a 1967 issue of a publication called Baking Industry *with no explanation of the origin of the name. Intrigued, I searched high and low for the "stream liner" reference to this cake, to no avail. I could only conclude that the cake might be named after the streamlined trains and automobiles of the early twentieth century, or possibly the lovely, sleek, and colorful art deco "streamliner" china made by the Salem China Company in the 1930s. Whatever the origin of its name, this luscious single-layer buttermilk cake is especially moist and light due to the addition of almond paste (see page 4). It's topped with a sunny lemon custard.*

8 to 10 servings	bake time	pan
	42 to 45 minutes	9 by 2-inch round cake pan, greased and bottom lined with a parchment paper circle

CUSTARD

Grated zest of 2 lemons

³/₄ cup whole milk

¹/₂ cup (3¹/₂ ounces) sugar

4 egg yolks

¹/₂ teaspoon fine sea salt

2 tablespoons cornstarch

¹/₂ cup lemon juice (from approximately 3 lemons)

¹/₂ cup (4 ounces) unsalted butter, cut into small cubes

CAKE

1¹/₄ cups (5 ounces) sifted cake flour

1¹/₂ teaspoons baking powder

¹/₂ teaspoon sea salt

³/₄ cup (6 ounces) almond paste, at room temperature

10 tablespoons (5 ounces) unsalted butter, at room temperature

²/₃ cup (4²/₃ ounces) sugar

3 tablespoons canola oil

2 teaspoons pure vanilla extract

3 eggs, at room temperature

²/₃ cup buttermilk, at room temperature

To make the lemon custard, combine the lemon zest, milk, and ¹/₄ cup of the sugar in a medium saucepan and heat over medium-low heat until just hot. Meanwhile, in a bowl, thoroughly whisk together the egg yolks, the remaining ¹/₄ cup of sugar, and the salt until well combined, then whisk in the cornstarch, then the lemon juice. Slowly whisk a third of the hot liquid into the yolk mixture. Pour the mixture back into the saucepan with the hot milk and cook over medium-low heat, whisking steadily, until the custard begins to thicken and bubble for 1 minute (you will need to stop whisking for a moment to check if it is bubbling). Strain the custard through a fine mesh sieve into a clean bowl and whisk in the butter until it has melted. Place a piece of plastic wrap directly upon the surface of the custard and place in the refrigerator to cool for about 2 hours. The custard is easiest to work with once it has set.

Center an oven rack and preheat the oven to 350°F.

To make the cake, sift together the flour, baking powder, and salt in a bowl, then whisk the mixture to ensure that the ingredients are well mixed.

Using a stand mixer with the paddle attachment, combine the almond paste, butter, sugar, canola oil, and vanilla on low speed until blended; gradually increase the speed to high and cream until very light and fluffy, 5 to 7 minutes, stopping the mixer frequently to scrape the paddle and the sides of the bowl with a rubber spatula. Blend in the eggs one at a time, adding the next one as soon as the previous one has disappeared into the batter. With the mixer on low speed, add the flour mixture in three parts,

continued

alternating with the buttermilk in two parts, beginning and ending with the flour. After each addition, mix until just barely blended and stop and scrape the bowl. Stop the mixer before the last of the flour has been incorporated and complete the blending by hand with a rubber spatula to ensure you do not overbeat the batter.

Pour the batter into the prepared pan and spread it evenly. Rap the pan firmly on the counter to release any air bubbles. Place the pan in the center of the oven and bake until the cake is a deep golden color and a wooden skewer poked in the middle comes out just barely clean, 42 to 45 minutes. The cake might crack on the surface as it bakes; don't worry, this simply provides a way for the cake to soak up more of the lemon custard.

Cool the cake in its pan on a wire rack for 30 minutes. Gently invert the cake onto the rack, leaving on the parchment paper until you assemble the cake. Flip the cake right side up and continue to cool the cake on the rack until it reaches room temperature.

To finish the cake, remove the parchment paper and place the cake right side up on a flat plate. Using a metal spatula, spread a thin layer of the lemon custard on the sides of the cake to seal the cake and give it a light shine. Put the rest of the lemon custard on top of the cake, spreading it just barely out to the edge. Use your spatula to make a swirly design in the custard on the top of the cake. Allow the assembled cake (or really, the lemon custard) to set in the refrigerator for 30 minutes.

Bring the cake to room temperature before serving (this will take about an hour). Any leftover cake keeps in an airtight container in the refrigerator for up to 3 days.

Blackberry Chocolate Cream Icebox Cake

Icebox cakes, later called refrigerator cakes, became popular in the 1930s and were all the rage by the 1950s. They were often made with lady fingers or wafers and always with whipped cream. Here, bake the thin, brown-sugar wafers, make the chocolate cream, then slather it on the wafers, chill, and serve. If you are in a hurry, substitute store-bought vanilla wafers in lieu of making your own. This is a traditional way to assemble an icebox cake. For an alternative, adapt the version on page 138 (it will yield fewer layers than the original recipe).

8 to 12 servings	bake time/wafers	pan
	15 minutes	A baking sheet lined with parchment paper

WAFERS

2 cups (10 ounces) all-purpose flour

³/₄ cup (5²/₃ ounces) firmly packed brown sugar

¹/₂ teaspoon baking powder

¹/₄ teaspoon fine sea salt

³/₄ cup (6 ounces) unsalted butter, cold, cut into cubes

3 tablespoons whole milk

1 teaspoon pure vanilla extract

CHOCOLATE CREAM

1 pint fresh blackberries

¹/₂ cup (2 ounces) lightly packed premium unsweetened Dutch-processed cocoa (see Cocoa Confusion, page 35)

¹/₂ cup (3¹/₂ ounces) sugar

2 cups heavy cream

1 tablespoon pure vanilla extract, or 2 tablespoons orange liqueur

Pinch of fine sea salt

To make the wafers, place the flour, brown sugar, baking powder, and salt together in a food processor and pulse several times until well combined. Drop the butter pieces into the bowl and whirl just until the mixture becomes coarse and crumbly. Add the milk and vanilla and process until the dough begins to clump around the sides of the bowl. Dump the dough onto a lightly floured surface and work the ingredients until the dough holds together. Shape the dough into a log roughly 8 inches long and 2 inches wide and place it onto a piece of parchment paper. Fold the paper over the dough and roll the log back and forth to smooth its surface. Wrap the log in the paper and transfer to the freezer to chill until hard, about 1 hour.

Center an oven rack and preheat the oven to 350°F.

With a large chef's knife and a ruler, slice the chilled wafer log into rounds ¹/₈ inch thick. Arrange the wafers 1 inch apart on a baking sheet lined with parchment paper. Bake the wafers until they are evenly golden brown, about 15 minutes. Slide the baked wafers on their parchment paper onto a wire rack to cool. Continue baking the wafers (lining the baking sheet with a new piece of parchment paper) until you have at least 28 of them; the recipe actually yields about twice that many (see below for what to do with the excess dough or wafers). Keep the unbaked sliced wafers chilled until they go into the oven.

To make the cream and assemble the cake, place a mixing bowl or the bowl of a stand mixer and its whisk attachment in the freezer for 5 minutes to chill. Set aside half the berries. With the back of a fork, smash the other half of the berries into a chunky puree in a bowl (you should have about $^3/_4$ cup of puree).

In the cold mixing bowl, whisk together the cocoa and sugar by hand and then mix in the cream on low speed. Increase the speed to high and whip the mixture to peaks that are just beyond soft but not yet stiff. Turn the mixer down to low speed to blend in the berry puree and vanilla or liqueur, followed by the salt. Gradually return the mixer to high speed and whip until stiff peaks just begin to form. It's best to err on the under-whipped side, since you can always give it a few strokes with a hand whisk if you need to thicken it up, but if it gets too stiff it can taste grainy.

Spread a generous tablespoonful of cream on top of a wafer and place it on a working surface. Repeat with a second wafer and set it atop the first wafer. Continue this process until you have a wafer tower that is 7 wafers tall, then build three more towers of the same height. Once you have made four towers, assemble the cake by laying the first tower on its side on a serving platter and then doing the same thing with the second tower, carefully pressing them close together side by side, and so on with the third and fourth towers, until you have a 7- by 4-cookie rectangular wedge. Frost the outside of the wedge with the remaining cream, cover it carefully with plastic wrap (using toothpicks, if they are handy, to prop up the plastic wrap so it does not come in contact with the top of the cake), and refrigerate for at least 12 hours. If during the assembly the cream warms and becomes too soft, pop it back in the refrigerator to chill and then rewhip it back to stiff peaks. Garnish with the reserved berries and serve chilled, sliced on the bias.

This cake gets a bit better with age! Keep it wrapped and refrigerated and it will be good for up to 4 days. The extra wafers, once baked, can be stored in an airtight container for up to a week or frozen for up to a month. Unbaked, the dough will last in the refrigerator for up to 5 days or in the freezer for up to 2 months.

How to Rescue Overwhipped Cream

Whipped cream is so heavenly when it is billowy and soft, but it can lose its luster when it is overwhipped, becoming grainy or stiff. To fix overwhipped cream, simply fold a tablespoon or two of cold unwhipped cream into the mixture.

Not-for-Children Gingerbread Bundt Cake

Bundt pans were originally made in the 1950s by an American company called Nordic Ware. It was only after home baker Ella Helfrich used a Bundt pan in 1966 for her second-prize-winning Tunnel of Fudge Cake in the 17th Pillsbury Bake-Off that Bundt pans leapt in popularity and began replacing the plain metal tube pans that had been the baking norm. This spicy gingerbread recipe is not for the faint of heart! Make the glaze as soon as you pop the cake into the oven, and your timing will be perfect.

12 servings	bake time	pan
	45 minutes	12-cup Bundt pan, greased

CAKE

¹/₃ cup (1¹/₂ ounces) lightly packed premium unsweetened Dutch-processed cocoa (see Cocoa Confusion, page 35)

¹/₂ teaspoon baking soda

1¹/₄ cups (15 ounces) unsulfured blackstrap molasses

1 cup brewed coffee

2³/₄ cups (13³/₄ ounces) all-purpose flour

1 teaspoon baking powder

1 teaspoon ground cinnamon

2 teaspoons ground ginger

¹/₂ teaspoon ground cloves

¹/₂ teaspoon fine sea salt

¹/₂ teaspoon ground black pepper

³/₄ cup (6 ounces) unsalted butter, at room temperature

1 cup (7¹/₂ ounces) firmly packed brown sugar

¹/₂ cup (3¹/₂ ounces) granulated sugar

¹/₂ cup canola oil

1 egg yolk, at room temperature

3 eggs, at room temperature

Center an oven rack and preheat the oven to 350°F.

To make the cake, in a medium-sized bowl, whisk the cocoa and baking soda together and stir in the molasses and the coffee. The mixture will bubble briefly.

In a separate bowl, sift together the flour, baking powder, cinnamon, ginger, cloves, salt, and pepper, then whisk by hand to ensure the ingredients are well mixed.

In the bowl of a stand mixer fitted with the paddle attachment, cream the butter and sugars together on medium-high speed until fluffy, about 5 minutes. As you make the batter, stop the mixer frequently and scrape the paddle and the sides of the bowl with a rubber spatula. With your mixer on low speed, drizzle the oil in until well combined. Blend in the egg yolk and eggs one at a time, adding the next one as soon as the previous one has disappeared into the batter. With the mixer still on low speed, add the flour mixture in three parts, alternating with the coffee/molasses mixture in two parts, beginning and ending with the flour. After each addition, mix until just barely blended and stop and scrape the bowl. Stop the mixer before the last of the flour has been incorporated and complete the blending by hand with a rubber spatula to ensure you do not overbeat the batter.

Pour the batter into the prepared pan. Bake in the middle of the oven until a toothpick or wooden skewer inserted in the middle of the cake comes out clean, about 45 minutes. Cool on a rack for 20 minutes before removing the cake from the pan. Continue to cool the cake on a wire rack until it reaches room temperature.

GLAZE

1/2 cup (3³/₄ ounces) firmly packed brown sugar

1/3 cup heavy whipping cream

1/4 cup (2 ounces) unsalted butter

Pinch of fine sea salt

1/3 cup (1¹/₃ ounces) sifted confectioners' sugar

2 tablespoons brandy

To make the glaze, combine the brown sugar, cream, butter, and salt in a small saucepan and boil for two minutes. While the mixture is boiling, resift the confectioners' sugar. Remove the glaze from the heat and add the sifted sugar. Whisk in the brandy. Let the glaze cool and thicken before pouring it over the cake.

Well wrapped and stored at room temperature, this cake keeps for up to 3 days.

Kentucky Bourbon Cake

Move over, shortcake! This buttermilk Bundt cake, drenched in a boozy bourbon glaze, is a great vehicle for whipped cream and strawberries. Kentucky Bourbon Cake was the prize-winning entry by Nell Lewis at the 1963 Pillsbury Bake-Off Contest in Platte City, Missouri.

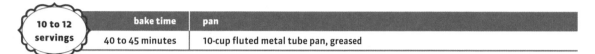

10 to 12 servings	bake time	pan
	40 to 45 minutes	10-cup fluted metal tube pan, greased

CAKE

3 cups (12 ounces) sifted cake flour

1 teaspoon baking powder

1/2 teaspoon baking soda

1 teaspoon fine sea salt

1 cup (8 ounces) unsalted butter

1 1/2 cups (10 1/2 ounces) sugar

1/2 cup (3 3/4 ounces) firmly packed brown sugar

4 eggs, at room temperature

1/4 cup bourbon

1 cup buttermilk, at room temperature

GLAZE

6 tablespoons (3 ounces) unsalted butter

3/4 cup (5 1/4 ounces) sugar

1/4 cup bourbon

Center an oven rack and preheat the oven to 350°F.

To make the cake, sift together the flour, baking powder, soda, and salt in a bowl, then whisk the mixture by hand to ensure that the ingredients are well mixed.

In the bowl of a stand mixer fitted with the paddle attachment, cream the butter and sugars together on medium-high speed until fluffy, about 5 minutes. As you make the batter, stop the mixer frequently and scrape the paddle and the sides of the bowl with a rubber spatula. Blend in the eggs one at a time. Combine the bourbon and buttermilk in a small bowl. With the mixer on low speed, add the flour mixture in three parts, alternating with the buttermilk-bourbon mixture in two parts, beginning and ending with the flour. After each addition, mix until just barely blended and stop and scrape the bowl. Stop the mixer before the last of the flour has been incorporated and complete the blending by hand with a rubber spatula.

Pour the batter into the prepared pan and spread it out evenly. Place the pan in the oven and bake until the cake is golden and springs back when touched, 40 to 45 minutes.

Make the glaze by combining the butter, sugar, and bourbon in a small saucepan over low heat just until the butter melts and the sugar dissolves, whisking to combine.

Remove the cake from the oven but leave it in the pan. Poke holes all over the top of the cake with a wooden skewer. Pour three-quarters of the glaze slowly over the cake, saving the remaining glaze. Allow the cake to cool for 30 minutes, then flip it out onto a serving plate so the glazed part is on the bottom. Brush the top with the remaining glaze. If the glaze has thickened, rewarm it over low heat.

The Harvey Wallbanger

The Harvey Wallbanger cocktail—a concoction of vodka, Galliano, and orange juice—was created in the early 1950s. By the early 1970s, a cake by the same name and with the same flavors was all the rage. Galliano is an Italian liqueur that is quite herbaceous; among its many ingredients are star anise, ginger, musk yarrow, lavender, juniper, peppermint, and vanilla. Although the alcohol bakes out of the cake, the sophisticated flavors (especially the overtone of vanilla) linger and meld perfectly with the citrus flavor in the cake.

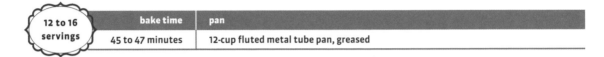

12 to 16 servings	bake time	pan
	45 to 47 minutes	12-cup fluted metal tube pan, greased

CAKE

2 cups (10 ounces) all-purpose flour

1 cup (4 ounces) sifted cake flour

2 teaspoons baking powder

1/2 teaspoon fine sea salt

1 cup (8 ounces) unsalted butter, at room temperature

2 cups (14 ounces) sugar

2 teaspoons pure vanilla extract

1/3 cup canola oil

5 eggs

1/2 cup orange juice

1/2 cup Galliano

1/4 cup vodka

GLAZE

1 1/2 cups (6 ounces) sifted confectioners' sugar

2 tablespoons orange juice

2 tablespoons Galliano

1 teaspoon vodka

Center an oven rack and preheat the oven to 350°F.

To make the cake, sift together the flours, baking powder, and salt in a bowl, then whisk the mixture by hand to ensure that the ingredients are well mixed.

Using a stand mixer fitted with the paddle attachment, cream the butter, sugar, and vanilla together on medium-high speed until fluffy, about 5 minutes. Reduce the speed to low and drizzle in the oil until incorporated. Return to medium-high speed and beat for another 2 minutes. Blend in the eggs one at a time, adding the next one just after the previous one is blended in. Stop the mixer frequently and scrape down the paddle, sides, and bottom of bowl to capture any escaping ingredients and ensure the batter is well combined. In a separate bowl, combine the orange juice, Galliano, and vodka. With the mixer on low speed, stir in the flour mixture in three parts, alternating with the orange juice cocktail in two parts, beginning and ending with the flour. Beat until just barely combined after each addition, scraping down the sides and bottom of the bowl between additions. Stop mixing just shy of complete incorporation and finish by hand with a rubber spatula.

Spread the batter in the prepared pan. Rap the pan firmly on the counter to release any air bubbles. Place the pan in the center of the oven and bake until the cake is golden in color and a wooden skewer poked in the middle comes out just barely clean, 45 to 47 minutes. Cool the cake in its pan on a wire rack for 30 minutes. Gently flip the cake out of its pan and lay it carefully back on the rack right side up.

To make the glaze, simply sift the confectioners' sugar into a bowl and whisk in the orange juice, Galliano, and vodka. If the glaze is too thick to pour over the cake, thin it by adding a teaspoon or two more of any of the three liquids. Glaze the cake while it is still warm to allow the glaze to soak into the cake. (Or, if you prefer the glaze to sit on top, wait for the cake to cool to room temperature before drizzling the glaze over it.)

When kept an airtight container at room temperature, this cake keeps for up to 5 days; it tastes better with age.

Little Cakes and Light Cakes

Turn to these recipes when your sweet tooth says it's time for a little something. This chapter contains irresistible little individual cakes, as well as cakes like angel food and chiffon that are known for their airy texture and light taste.

Once only a sideshow to layer cakes, cupcakes have taken center stage, as demonstrated by the many cupcake shops in Portland, New York, and other cities. I've included a few old-time cupcake recipes here: Malted Milk Chocolate Cupcakes (page 57), which give a nod to the craze in the early twentieth century for malted milkshakes; Tropicups (page 58), a recipe developed in the 1950s when pineapples became commercially available; and Mississippi Mud Cupcakes with Marshmallow Frosting (page 55), a miniature version of the chocolate-pecan-marshmallow cake that was popular in the 1960s. Although I've only included a handful of cupcake recipes in this book, you can make cupcakes out of virtually any cake batter, provided you knock 15 to 20 minutes off the baking time. The Cherry Chip Cake (page 133), for example, makes divine cupcakes!

A couple of other individual-serving cakes have made their way into this chapter as well. For an elegant dessert, try the Lemon Queen Cakes with their billowy meringue topping (page 50). And the indulgent Boston Cream Pie-lets (page 53) shouldn't be missed if you, like me, favor the pudding over the cake.

Angel food cakes and chiffon cakes both grew in popularity in the 1930s, once American households had ovens with reliable temperatures and electric mixers that could whip egg whites with ease. Both of these appliances were quite important to the success of cakes dependent on fluffy egg whites and air! For a light cake that contains some of my favorite flavors, whip up the Maple Pecan Chiffon Cake with Brown Butter Icing (page 63). For a zesty twist on a retro favorite, try the Daffodil Cake (page 60). And if find yourself with an abundance of egg whites, try your hand at the Angel Cake with Chocolate and Orange Freckles (page 64). (Don't forget: leftover angel food cake is delicious toasted the next day.)

Lemon Queen Cakes with Meringue Frosting

These fun little cakes are a three-tiered treat: a billowy meringue on top, cake in the middle, and a moist lemon pudding hidden on the bottom. In the 1700s, small cakes—including "queen cakes," a name for individual-serving pound cakes—were commonly baked in teacups. By the 1800s, these cakes were better known as "cup cakes." Be sure you use ovenproof teacups, not your grandmother's finest china! If you don't know if your teacups can handle the heat, use ramekins instead.

6 to 8 servings	bake time	pan
	30 to 32 minutes	6 to 8 teacups or ramekins (4 to 6 ounces each), greased with about 2 tablespoons of soft butter, plus a roasting pan large enough to hold all the cups

CAKE

¼ cup (2 ounces) unsalted butter, at room temperature

1⅓ cups (9⅓ ounces) sugar

2 tablespoons grated lemon zest (from approximately 2 lemons)

4 eggs, separated

½ cup lemon juice (from approximately 3 lemons)

¾ cup (3¾ ounces) all-purpose flour

1¼ cups whole milk

¼ teaspoon fine sea salt

MERINGUE TOPPING

4 egg whites (see Whipping Egg Whites, page 87)

1 cup (7 ounces) sugar

⅛ teaspoon fine sea salt

Center an oven rack and preheat the oven to 350°F.

Butter the teacups and place them in a roasting pan.

To make the cake, in the bowl of a stand mixer fitted with the paddle attachment, beat the butter, sugar, and lemon zest on medium speed until well combined. Add the egg yolks, two at a time, and blend on medium-high speed until the batter is creamy. Scrape the sides and bottom of the bowl often to keep the mixture uniform. Stop the mixer and use a rubber spatula to stir in the lemon juice by hand, followed by the flour, mixing until evenly incorporated. Finish the batter by stirring in the milk. The mixture should be thin.

In a clean bowl, whisk the egg whites and salt until medium peaks form. Gently fold the egg whites into the lemon mixture until all of the ingredients are evenly incorporated. Distribute the batter among the buttered teacups, filling them to just below the rim. Place the roasting pan in the oven and carefully add enough hot water to the pan to come about one-third of the way up the sides of the cups. Bake the cakes until the tops of the cups are firm and appear golden in spots with little cracks beginning to form, 30 to 32 minutes. (The bottoms of the cakes will stay a pudding-like consistency, so don't try to test for doneness using a wooden skewer.) Carefully remove the teacups from the pan and place them on a wire rack to cool.

Once the cakes have cooled, prepare the meringue topping. In the bowl of a stand mixer, whisk by hand the egg whites, sugar, and salt. Place the bowl over (not in) a saucepan of simmering water. Continue to gently whisk

continued

the mixture by hand until it reaches 160°F. (Use a thermometer; if you don't have one, proceed carefully by feel: the whites need to get extremely hot—too hot to touch!) Move the bowl to the stand mixer and using the whisk attachment, whip the whites on medium-high speed until they have tripled in volume, hold stiff peaks, and look thick and glossy. Quickly distribute the meringue evenly atop the cakes, spreading the meringue over each to completely hide the lemon cake beneath. Using a metal spatula or the back of a metal spoon, sculpt the top of the meringue into peaks and valleys.

Use a kitchen torch to toast the meringue to a golden brown hue (alternatively, place the cups on a baking tray and slide the tray into the middle of the oven preheated to broil, watching vigilantly and turning the tray as necessary to toast the meringue tops).

Because the egg whites in the meringue cooked to 160°F, these cakes can sit at room temperature for up to 2 days. That being said, this dessert tastes best on the day it is made!

Boston Cream Pie-lets

Boston cream pie is not a pie at all. It's a cake with a generous vanilla pudding interior and a chocolate ganache exterior. And for me, the vanilla pudding is what it's all about! Rather than make one big cake, I've redesigned this recipe to make "pie-lets": small individual cakes, served in pudding cups or champagne coupes. This presentation can hold a lot more pudding than the amount you typically find sandwiched between the layers of a Boston cream pie, which is never enough for me! Boston's Parker House Hotel takes credit for creating this dessert in the mid-nineteenth century. Back then, cakes were often baked in pie tins instead of cake pans, which may be how the cake got its name.

8 servings	bake time	pan
	28 to 32 minutes	Eight 6-ounce pudding cups, plus a greased 13 by 9-inch baking dish

CAKE

2 cups (8 ounces) sifted cake flour

2 teaspoons baking powder

1 teaspoon fine sea salt

1½ cups heavy cream, cold

1¼ cups (8¾ ounces) sugar

3 eggs

2 teaspoons pure vanilla extract

PUDDING

1 vanilla bean

4 cups whole milk

1 cup (7 ounces) sugar

8 egg yolks

½ teaspoon fine sea salt

¼ cup (1 ounce) cornstarch (see Magic of Cornstarch, page 137)

4 tablespoons (2 ounces) unsalted butter, cut into cubes

¾ cup warm Chocolate Ganache (page 146)

Center an oven rack and preheat the oven to 350°F.

To make the cake, sift together the cake flour, baking powder, and salt in a bowl, then whisk the ingredients by hand to ensure they are well mixed.

Using a stand mixer fitted with the whisk attachment, whip the cream on high speed until soft, droopy peaks form. On medium-low speed, add the sugar in a steady stream and then return the mixer to high speed to continue to whip the cream until stiff peaks begin to form. Return the mixer to low speed and add the eggs one a time, followed by the vanilla. Stir in the flour mixture in three parts, adding the next addition as soon as the flour has been incorporated. Turn off the mixer before all the flour is completely mixed into the batter and finish mixing the batter by hand with a rubber spatula. Pour the batter into the prepared baking dish and place it in the center of the oven until the cake springs back in the middle when lightly pressed, 28 to 32 minutes. Cool the cake in its pan on a wire rack until it reaches room temperature.

While the cake is in the oven, make the pudding. With a small paring knife, split the vanilla bean in half lengthwise, scrape out the seeds from the pod, and put them, along with the pod, into a large saucepan. Add the milk and ⅓ cup of the sugar and place the pan over medium-low heat until the milk is hot but not boiling. While the milk is heating, in a small bowl thoroughly whisk together the yolks, the remaining ⅔ cup of sugar, and the salt, then blend in the cornstarch. Slowly whisk a third of the hot milk into the yolk mixture. Pour this mixture back into the saucepan with

continued

the remaining hot milk and gently cook over medium-low heat, whisking steadily, until the pudding just begins to thicken and has been bubbling for roughly 1 minute (you will need to stop whisking for a moment to check if it is bubbling). Strain the mixture through a fine mesh sieve into a clean bowl and whisk in the butter until melted.

To assemble the pie-lets, use a $2^3/_4$-inch round biscuit or cookie cutter to cut out 8 miniature cakes directly from the pan. Carefully remove the miniature cakes from the pan and, with a serrated knife, cut them in half horizontally to create 2 layers per cake. (Set aside the leftover cake to snack on later.) Spoon 3 tablespoons of warm pudding into the bottom of each pudding dish. Set the bottom half of the miniature cake into the pudding, then spoon on another 3 tablespoons of pudding and cover it with the top half of the cake. Cover the pie-lets with plastic wrap and refrigerate for at least 4 hours to set up. Once the pie-lets have firmed up, spoon 2 table-spoons of warm chocolate ganache over each cake and allow the dessert to sit at room temperature for 30 minutes before serving.

Well wrapped and refrigerated, pie-lets keep for up to 5 days. Try to hold off on glazing the cakes with ganache until just before serving them. Ganache tends to dull in color when cold, though the flavor will not be affected in any way.

Mississippi Mud Cupcakes with Marshmallow Frosting

I can't make these cupcakes without humming "Mississippi Mud," a 1927 song originally sung by Bing Crosby and recorded by numerous artists over the years. Mississippi mud pie and Mississippi mud cake, two dense chocolate creations from the 1960s, traditionally called for chocolate, pecans, and marshmallows. I've revised the recipe to make rich chocolate cupcakes embedded with pecans and frosted with a decadent marshmallow frosting. Both the cupcakes and the marshmallow frosting are easy and fast to make.

24 cupcakes	bake time	pan
	20 minutes	Muffin tins for 24 standard (¹/₃-cup) cupcakes, lined with paper cups

1 cup hot coffee (left over from the morning brew is fine)

³/₄ cup (3 ounces) lightly packed premium unsweetened Dutch-processed cocoa (see Cocoa Confusion, page 35)

2 cups (10 ounces) all-purpose flour

2 cups (14 ounces) sugar

1 teaspoon baking powder

1 teaspoon fine sea salt

¹/₂ teaspoon baking soda

1 cup (4 ounces) toasted chopped pecans (see Toasting Nuts, page 114)

1 cup (6¹/₂ ounces) semisweet chocolate chips

2 eggs, at room temperature

1 cup buttermilk, at room temperature

¹/₂ cup canola oil

2 teaspoons pure vanilla extract

Marshmallow Frosting (page 155)

Center an oven rack and preheat the oven to 350°F.

In a small bowl, whisk the hot coffee into the cocoa. Set aside to cool.

Sift together the flour, sugar, baking powder, salt, and baking soda in a large bowl. Whisk the mixture together by hand to ensure that the ingredients are well mixed, then stir in the pecans and chocolate chips.

In a separate bowl, whisk together the eggs, buttermilk, oil, vanilla, and cooled cocoa mixture. Add the wet ingredients to the dry ingredients and stir the batter together with a rubber spatula until just combined (too much mixing will cause the tops of the cupcakes to be unevenly domed). Pour the batter evenly among the prepared cupcake tins (approximately 2¹/₃ ounces per cupcake), filling each well three-quarters full. Place the cupcake tins in the middle rack of the preheated oven and bake until the cupcakes have domed on top and bounce back when lightly pressed, about 20 minutes. Cool the cakes in their tins on a wire rack. Once the cupcakes have cooled, remove them from their tins and pipe a mound of marshmallow frosting on each.

These cupcakes keep for 3 days in an airtight container at room temperature.

Malted Milk Chocolate Cupcakes

Malted milk powder first arrived on the scene in 1897 as a health aid, but soon became a popular ingredient in chocolate milkshakes at the Walgreen's pharmacy soda fountains in Chicago. More than one hundred years later, here's my recipe for malted milk chocolate cupcakes. You can usually find malted milk powder in the baking aisle of your local grocery store (though sometimes it's on the shelf next to the cocoa and coffee). A few things to note: the frosting will take about three hours to make from start to finish, so plan accordingly. Also, use paper cupcake cups and your cupcakes will be perky and presentable; without them, the cupcakes turn out on the flatter side.

24 cupcakes	bake time	pan
	24 to 26 minutes	Muffin tins for 24 standard (¹/₃-cup) cupcakes, lined with paper cups

2 cups (10 ounces) all-purpose flour

2 cups (14 ounces) sugar

2 teaspoons baking powder

1 teaspoon fine sea salt

1 cup (5 ounces) malted milk powder (not Ovaltine)

6 ounces unsweetened chocolate, chopped

¹/₂ cup (4 ounces) unsalted butter

¹/₄ cup canola oil

1³/₄ cups whole milk, at room temperature

3 eggs, at room temperature

2 teaspoons pure vanilla extract

Malted Milk Chocolate Frosting (page 150)

24 malted milk balls for garnish (optional)

Center an oven rack and preheat the oven to 350°F.

In the bowl of a stand mixer, sift together the flour, sugar, baking powder, and salt. Add the malted milk powder and whisk the mixture by hand to ensure that the ingredients are well mixed.

Melt the chocolate and butter in a heat-resistant bowl set over a pot of simmering water. Once both are melted, remove the bowl from the heat and stir in the oil until the mixture is uniform. Scrape the chocolate mixture into the bowl of dry ingredients, pour in 1 cup of the milk, and blend with the paddle attachment on low speed until incorporated, scraping the bottom well to incorporate any dry-ingredient patches. Once combined, kick up the mixer to medium-high speed for 1 minute. Stop the mixer and scrape the paddle, sides, and bottom of the bowl. Whisk together the remaining ³/₄ cup of milk, the eggs, and the vanilla in a separate bowl and add half this mixture into the batter on low speed. Scrape down the sides of the bowl and add the second half of the mixture, blending until well combined.

Pour the thin batter into the paper-lined pans, filling the cups to just below the rim. Place the tins in the middle of the oven and bake until the cupcakes are perky and firm on the top, 24 to 26 minutes. Cool the cakes in their tins on a wire rack until they reach room temperature.

Once cool, frost the cupcakes with the frosting and place a malted milk ball on top for decoration.

These cupcakes are best the day they are made but keep for 3 days in an airtight container at room temperature.

Tropicups

We can thank James Dole for popularizing the pineapple in the early twentieth century. I found a recipe for pineapple and coconut "Tropicups" in a 1953 Bakers Weekly *baking journal—back in the day when "cup cake" was two words, and "cocoanut" was the common spelling for coconut. The journal touted the cupcake's form as "one that could stand considerable promotion and glamorizing (if we may use that term) as it is often taken too much for granted." In the interest of glamorizing—or at least, promoting—cupcakes, I have revived the recipe for Tropicups. The unsweetened grated coconut you want for these is sometimes known as "macaroon cut," and it's often found in the bulk bins. Use coconut milk, not cream of coconut, and remember to shake the can vigorously before you open it to blend the separated cream and liquid.*

24 cupcakes	bake time	pan
	23 to 25 minutes	Muffin tins for 24 standard (¹/₃-cup) cupcakes, wells greased with about 2 tablespoons of soft unsalted butter

CUPCAKES

1¹/₂ cups (6 ounces) lightly packed sweetened shredded coconut

3 cups (15 ounces) all-purpose flour

1 tablespoon baking powder

1 teaspoon ground nutmeg

1 teaspoon fine sea salt

1 cup (3 ounces) lightly packed unsweetened grated coconut

1³/₄ cups (12¹/₄ ounces) sugar

³/₄ cup (6 ounces) unsalted butter, at room temperature

6 ounces cream cheese, at room temperature

2 teaspoons pure vanilla extract

4 eggs, at room temperature

One 14-ounce can crushed unsweetened pineapple, with juice

Center an oven rack and preheat oven to 350°F.

To prepare the cupcake tins, rub each cupcake well with a smear of butter and place 1 teaspoon of sweetened shredded coconut in the bottom of each well.

Sift together the flour, baking powder, nutmeg, and salt in a bowl. Add the unsweetened grated coconut and whisk the mixture by hand to ensure that the ingredients are well mixed.

In the bowl of a stand mixer fitted with the paddle attachment, blend the sugar, butter, and cream cheese on low speed. Increase the speed to medium-high and blend until fluffy, about 5 minutes, stopping the machine and scraping the bowl and paddle down as needed to keep the mixture uniform. Add the eggs one at a time, mixing until just incorporated between additions, followed by the vanilla. On low speed, stir in the flour mixture in three additions, alternating with the pineapple in two additions, beginning and ending with the flour mixture and scraping down the sides of the bowl occasionally. The batter will be thick.

Using a spoon or an ice cream scoop, scoop equal amounts of the batter into the prepared cupcake wells (approximately ¹/₄ cup of batter for each well), so that the center of the mound is slightly higher than the top edge of the well. Place the cupcake tins on the middle rack of the preheated oven and bake until the cupcakes are firm on top (they should be blond and just

GLAZE

2 cups (8 ounces) sifted confectioners' sugar

$1/3$ cup coconut milk

1 teaspoon pure vanilla extract

slightly golden around the edges after 23 to 25 minutes). Cool the cakes in their tins on a wire rack.

While the oven is still on, place the remainder of the shredded coconut on a baking sheet and toast it in the oven for 10 minutes, giving it a gentle nudge after 5 minutes to encourage even browning.

Once the cupcakes have cooled slightly, poke 6 to 8 holes in the top of each cupcake with a wooden skewer.

To make the glaze, sift the confectioners' sugar into a small bowl. Whisk in the coconut milk and vanilla. Dip the top of each cupcake into the glaze, holding the cupcake over the glaze long enough to allow the excess glaze to drip off before sprinkling the cupcake with the toasted coconut. Allow about 20 minutes for the glaze to set before serving.

In an airtight container at room temperature, these cupcakes keep for 3 days.

Daffodil Cake

A cheery tribute to spring, this light cake is a yellow-and-white marbled angel food cake that dates back at least to the 1930s, when a recipe for Daffodil Cake was published in a Better Homes and Gardens *cookbook. This recipe calls for a tequila lime glaze (my mind naturally wanders to margaritas when I am juicing limes), but if you'd prefer to omit the tequila and up the amount of lime juice, this cake will taste just as good. The recipe also calls for lime oil, which heightens the cake's flavor.*

8 to 10 servings	bake time	pan
	40 to 45 minutes	10-inch straight-sided metal tube pan or angel food cake pan with feet, ungreased

CAKE

1 cup (4 ounces) sifted cake flour

1¹/₃ cup (5¹/₃ ounces) sifted confectioners' sugar

1 cup (7 ounces) granulated sugar

Grated zest of 2 limes

6 egg yolks

¹/₂ teaspoon lime oil

12 egg whites

¹/₂ teaspoon fine sea salt

1 teaspoon cream of tartar

TEQUILA LIME GLAZE

1¹/₂ cups (6 ounces) sifted confectioners' sugar

2 tablespoons lime juice

2 tablespoons tequila

Adjust a rack to the bottom third of the oven and preheat the oven to 350°F.

Whisk the cake flour and confectioners' sugar together in a bowl and then sift the mixture three times (yes, three times!) and set it aside. In a small bowl, blend ³/₄ cup of the granulated sugar with the lime zest (for the best results, rub the zest into the sugar with your clean hands to distribute it evenly). In a bowl of a stand mixer fitted with the whisk attachment, blend the yolks, the remaining ¹/₄ cup of granulated sugar, and the lime oil for 3 minutes on high speed. Pour the yolk mixture into a separate large bowl and set aside.

Meticulously clean the bowl and whisk attachment to whip the egg whites (see page 87). Starting on low speed, whip the whites with the salt on medium speed until frothy. Add the cream of tartar and whip on high speed until soft peaks form. On low speed, gradually add the lime-sugar, about 3 tablespoons at a time. Return to high speed and whip until peaks form that are just beyond soft but are not yet stiff. Remove the bowl from the mixer and sift one-third of the flour mixture over the whites and, using a rubber spatula, gently fold the flour into the whites with as few strokes as possible. Add the rest of the flour mixture in two additions, sifting and then folding only until evenly incorporated. Gently fold half of the egg white batter into the sugared yolks.

You should now have one bowl of yellow batter and one bowl of white batter. Using your rubber spatula, gently drop alternating dollops of yellow and white batter into the ungreased tube pan until you run out of batter. Lightly tap the pan on the counter to loosen any large air bubbles. Place the cake in the bottom third of the oven and bake until the top is golden and springs back when lightly touched, 40 to 45 minutes, paying close attention to the center to confirm the batter is set near the inner sides of the tube. Remove the cake from the oven and let it cool upside down by inverting the cake pan onto its legs (if it has them) or by inverting the pan over a cup or the neck of a bottle. Let the cake cool for at least 2 hours. To unmold the cake, turn it right side up and insert a skinny knife or thin metal spatula around the edge of the pan to free the cake from the sides. Then invert the cake onto a plate.

To make the glaze, sift the confectioners' sugar into a bowl and whisk in the lime juice and tequila. If the glaze is too thick, add a teaspoon or two more of either liquid. Pour the glaze over the top of the cake, letting it drip down the sides. Once glazed, the cake should sit at room temperature for about 30 minutes before serving.

This cake is best if eaten within a few hours of cooling. Any leftover cake can be stored in a cake keeper at cool room temperature for up to 2 days.

Maple Pecan Chiffon Cake with Brown Butter Icing

Chiffon cakes are made with oil instead of butter. Harry Baker, a Los Angeles insurance salesman and recreational cook credited with developing chiffon cake in the 1920s. He then sold his recipe to General Mills in the 1940s, whereupon Betty Crocker popularized chiffon cakes as the "first new cake in a hundred years."

8 to 10 servings	bake time	pan
	50 to 55 minutes	10-inch angel food cake pan with feet, bottom lined with parchment paper, ungreased

2¼ cups (9 ounces) sifted cake flour

2 teaspoons baking powder

1 teaspoon fine sea salt

¾ cup (5⅔ ounces) firmly packed dark brown sugar

6 egg yolks

½ cup canola oil

½ cup pure maple syrup

¼ cup water

1 tablespoon pure vanilla extract

8 egg whites, at room temperature (see Whipping Egg Whites, page 87)

½ teaspoon cream of tartar

½ cup (3½ ounces) granulated sugar

½ cup (2 ounces) toasted finely chopped pecans (see Toasting Nuts, page 114)

Brown Butter Icing (page 154)

Adjust a rack to the bottom third of the oven and preheat the oven to 325°F.

In a large bowl, sift together the cake flour, baking powder, and salt. Add the brown sugar and whisk the mixture by hand to combine.

In a small bowl, whisk together the yolks, oil, maple syrup, water, and vanilla. Add the liquid ingredients to the dry mixture and briskly stir with a rubber spatula until just smooth. Do not overmix.

In the clean bowl of a stand mixer fitted with the whisk attachment, whip the egg whites on medium speed until foamy. Add the cream of tartar and whip on high speed until soft peaks form. Turn the mixer down to medium speed and gradually add the sugar in a steady stream. Kick the mixer up to high speed and whip until the whites just hold firm (not stiff!) glossy peaks.

Fold a third of the whites into the batter using as few strokes as possible. Add the remaining whites, folding only until evenly incorporated. Lightly fold in the pecans during the last few strokes. Gently pour the batter into the prepared pan and bake until the top springs back when touched or a toothpick inserted in the middle comes out with a few crumbs attached, 50 to 55 minutes.

Remove the cake from the oven and let it cool upside down by inverting the cake pan onto its legs. To remove the cooled cake from the pan, slide a long thin knife or spatula along the sides to loosen and knock the pan sharply on a hard surface until the cake drops out.

Frost the top and sides with brown butter icing. To cut the cake, use an angel food cake cutter or a serrated knife and a sawing (rather than a slicing) motion. Store in an airtight container for up to 3 days.

Angel Cake with Chocolate and Orange Freckles

Angel food cakes, also called angel cakes, made their appearance in the late nineteenth century but became more popular after 1930, once Sunbeam introduced the Mixmaster, the first affordable stand mixer. The key to whipping up a light and airy angel cake is to stop your mixer when the whites are just shy of stiff peaks (I call them "firm peaks") and gently fold the well-sifted, practically weightless dry ingredients into them. Serve this cake with lightly sweetened whipped cream and fresh berries; a seasonal fruit curd would also be delicious.

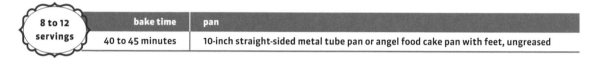

8 to 12 servings	bake time	pan
	40 to 45 minutes	10-inch straight-sided metal tube pan or angel food cake pan with feet, ungreased

3 ounces bittersweet chocolate, in bar form

1 cup (4 ounces) sifted cake flour

1 cup (4 ounces) sifted confectioners' sugar

12 egg whites, at room temperature (see Whipping Egg Whites, page 87)

1/2 teaspoon fine sea salt

1 teaspoon cream of tartar

1¼ cups (8¾ ounces) granulated sugar

2 teaspoons pure vanilla extract

Grated zest of 1 orange

Place the chocolate in the freezer for 5 minutes before grating it coarsely with a cheese grater. Set aside at room temperature.

Adjust a rack to the bottom third of the oven and preheat the oven to 350°F.

Whisk together the cake flour and confectioners' sugar in a bowl, then sift the mixture together three times.

In the clean bowl of a stand mixer fitted with the clean whisk attachment, whisk the egg whites and salt on medium speed until foamy. Add the cream of tartar and whip on high speed until soft peaks just begin to form. Turn the mixer down to medium speed and gradually add the granulated sugar in a steady stream. Kick the mixer back up to high speed and whip until firm (not stiff) peaks form. Reduce the speed to low, add the vanilla and the orange zest, and mix until these are just incorporated.

Transfer the whites to a wide bowl and sift one-third of the flour mixture over the whites. Using a rubber spatula, fold the flour into the whites with as few strokes as possible. Add the rest of the flour mixture in two additions, sifting and folding only until evenly incorporated. As you fold in the last addition of flour, add and fold in the grated chocolate. Pour the batter into the pan. Slowly run a knife in a zigzag motion through the mixture to break up any large air pockets. Place the pan in the bottom third of the oven and bake until the top is golden and springs back when lightly touched, 40 to 45 minutes. Remove the cake from the oven and let it cool upside down by inverting the cake pan onto its legs (if it has them) or by inverting the pan over a cup or the neck of a bottle. Let the cake cool for at least $1^1/_2$ hours. To remove the cooled cake from the pan, loosen the sides with a long thin knife or spatula and knock the pan sharply on a hard surface until the cake drops out.

To cut the cake, use an angel food cake cutter or serrated knife and a sawing (rather than a slicing) motion.

This cake is best served within 12 hours of cooling. Any leftovers should be covered with a tea towel and kept at room temperature.

Angel Food Cake Cutters

Angel food cake cutters were once common in American homes. The tool gently separates pieces of cake using comb tines instead of a solid knife blade, thereby cutting angel food and sponge cakes without crushing them.

Flips and Rolls

Technique is what knits this chapter of old fashioned upside-down cakes and elegant cake rolls together. At first peek, these pages could intimidate even the best of bakers. Fear not: take a deep breath and seize hold of your confidence, because these recipes are designed to be as easy to make as possible, and will soon have you flipping and rolling like a pro.

There's nothing I like more than taking fruit at the peak of its season and baking it up into a dessert. Upside-down cakes are just the thing to showcase the flavor of fruit, whether it's the tang of rhubarb in White Chocolate Rhubarb Downside-Up Cake (page 80), the tart complexity of fresh apricots in Chocolate Apricot Upside-Down Cake (page 79), or the simple pleasure of a summer nectarine in Nectarine Oat Upside-Down Cake (page 68). Upside-down cakes can be as fitting on a table dressed with linen as on a picnic table. It's up to you whether you scatter the fruit randomly in its buttery caramel or place it artfully in a pattern to create a design on what will become the top of your upside-down cake.

Cake rolls appear to have fallen out of fashion, yet they are so simple and ever so elegant. It is my quest to bring them back to the dessert table! While the spiral cakes in this chapter may seem daunting to those who have never tried to make a cake roll, they are actually not difficult so long as you follow the directions to the letter. These cakes are basically sponge cakes coupled with a flavored cream filling, rolled, and then sliced and served in a cross-section. For a decadent treat, try the Butterscotch Cream Roll-Up (page 71) with its homemade butterscotch sauce.

Nectarine Oat Upside-Down Cake

This dessert is as much fruit as it is cake. Look for freestone nectarines, which arrive later in the season. Not nectarine season? Try apricots, pears, or apples instead. The base of this dessert is a moist buttermilk cake, with the addition of oat flour. The rolled oats in this recipe are optional; they add a hearty texture to the bottom of the cake.

8 to 10 servings	bake time	pan
	55 to 60 minutes	9 by 2-inch square pan, sides and bottom greased with 1 tablespoon of soft unsalted butter, then lined with parchment paper greased with a bit more butter

TOPPING

2 pounds yellow-fleshed nectarines (approximately 4 large or 6 small), washed, pitted, and each sliced into 8 pieces

3/4 cup (5 1/4 ounces) sugar

1/4 cup (2 ounces) unsalted butter

CAKE

1 1/4 cups (6 1/4 ounces) all-purpose flour

3/4 cup (3 ounces) sifted oat flour

1 1/2 teaspoons baking powder

1 teaspoon fine sea salt

3/4 cup (6 ounces) unsalted butter, at room temperature

1 cup (7 ounces) sugar

2 eggs, at room temperature

2 teaspoons pure vanilla extract

1 cup buttermilk, at room temperature

1/4 cup (1 ounce) rolled oats (optional)

Whipped cream, for serving (optional)

To make the topping, gently toss the nectarines with the sugar in a bowl and let sit for at least 30 minutes to draw out some of the juices. Strain the juice into a sauté pan, letting the strainer sit for about 10 minutes to collect all of the juice. Reserve the nectarines. Add the butter to the juices in the pan and cook over medium heat until the butter melts and the juices simmer down into a rosy caramel syrup, stirring occasionally to avoid any hot spots. This can take anywhere from 7 to 10 minutes, depending on how juicy your fruit is. Pour the syrup into the prepared cake pan and spread it out to the sides as best you can. Set it aside to cool for a few minutes before arranging the nectarines on top of the caramel. If the fruit is on the larger size, try laying three rows of overlapping slices in the square pan (not a necessary step, of course, as it all tastes the same in the end).

Adjust a rack to the bottom third of the oven and preheat the oven to 350°F.

To make the cake, sift together the flours, baking powder, and salt in a bowl and then whisk the mixture by hand to ensure all the ingredients are well mixed.

In the bowl of a stand mixer fitted with the paddle attachment, cream the butter and sugar together on medium-high speed until fluffy, about 5 minutes. As you make the batter, stop the mixer frequently and scrape the paddle and the sides of the bowl with a rubber spatula. Blend in the eggs one at a time, adding the next one as soon as the previous one has disappeared into the batter, then blend in the vanilla. With the mixer on low speed, add the flour mixture in three parts, alternating with the buttermilk in two parts, beginning and ending with the flour. After each addition, mix until just barely blended and stop and scrape the bowl. Stop the mixer before the last of the flour has been incorporated and complete the blending by hand with a rubber spatula to ensure you do not overbeat the batter.

Spoon the batter over the nectarines and evenly spread it out to the sides of the pan. Sprinkle the oats evenly over the batter. Rap the pan lightly on the counter to settle the batter, then place the pan in the bottom third of the oven. Bake until the cake is lightly golden and slightly cracked, and a toothpick inserted into the top half of the cake comes out just moist with crumbs, 55 to 60 minutes. Cool the cake in its pan on a wire rack for an hour, then invert the cake onto a plate, leaving the pan on top of the cake until you are ready to serve it (this conserves heat). When you are ready to serve, lift the pan off the cake and peel off the parchment paper. Serve this cake warm with a dollop of whipped cream for dessert or unadorned for breakfast.

This cake is best the day it is made, but any leftovers keep in an airtight container (or under a cake dome) at room temperature for up to 2 days.

Oat Flour

If your local grocery does not stock oat flour, you can make your own by grinding whole oats—not instant—in a clean coffee grinder. Oat flour is best kept in an airtight container in the freezer. It is a great addition to pancakes or any other baking (simply replace no more than a quarter of the flour with oat flour).

Butterscotch Cream Roll-Up

What dessert isn't better with an authentic butterscotch sauce? Here, almonds add a desirable crunch to this lovely chiffon butterscotch roll. If you prefer a traditional spiral log, see the directions for rolling the Coffee Crunch Spiral (page 77).

10 to 12 servings	bake time	pan
	22 to 25 minutes	12 by 16-inch jelly roll pan: grease the pan with baking spray, line it with parchment paper, spray the parchment paper, then dust it with flour and tap out any excess. Don't skip these steps or the rolling may be difficult.

BUTTERSCOTCH SAUCE

1/3 cup (3 ounces) unsalted butter

1 cup (7 1/2 ounces) firmly packed dark brown sugar

1 cup heavy cream

1 tablespoon whisky

1 1/2 teaspoons pure vanilla extract

1/2 teaspoon fine sea salt

CAKE

1 cup (4 ounces) sifted cake flour

1 cup (7 ounces) sugar

1 teaspoon baking powder

1/2 teaspoon fine sea salt

1/2 cup canola oil

4 egg yolks, at room temperature

1/4 cup water

1 teaspoons pure vanilla extract

6 egg whites, at room temperature (see Whipping Egg Whites, page 87)

1/4 teaspoon cream of tartar

FILLING

1 1/2 cups heavy cream, cold

Heaping 1/2 cup (2 ounces) natural sliced almonds, toasted (see Toasting Nuts, page 114)

To make the butterscotch sauce, melt the butter over medium heat in a large heavy-bottomed saucepan. Dump in the brown sugar all at once and stir with a wooden spoon to combine. Cook, stirring frequently, until the mixture begins to simmer and changes from a wet sand consistency to a liquid that gives off a lovely molasses smell and looks like taffy, approximately 3 minutes from the time it comes to a simmer. Drizzle 1/4 cup of the cream into the mixture and vigorously blend the cream into the sugar and whisk in the remaining cream. Turn the heat up to medium-high and allow the sauce to boil, whisking occasionally, until it has darkened, about 8 minutes. Remove the pot from the heat and allow the sauce to cool for a few minutes before adding the whisky, vanilla, and salt. Refrigerate until cold.

Center an oven rack and preheat the oven to 325°F.

To make the cake, sift together the flour, baking powder, salt, and 3/4 cup of the sugar in a large bowl, then whisk the ingredients by hand. In a small bowl, whisk together the oil, yolks, water, and vanilla. Add the liquid mixture to the dry ingredients and briskly stir with a rubber spatula until just smooth.

In the clean bowl of a stand mixer fitted with the clean whisk attachment, whip the egg whites on medium speed until frothy. Add the cream of tartar and gradually increase the speed to high, whipping until the whites just form a soft peak. With the mixer on medium speed, gradually add the remaining 1/4 cup of sugar in a slow stream. Return the mixer to high and continue whipping until the whites just begin to hold firm, shiny peaks.

With a rubber spatula, fold a third of the whites into the batter, using as few strokes as possible. Add the remaining whites, folding until

continued

incorporated. Pour the batter into the prepared pan and smooth the top (this is best done with an offset spatula). Place the pan in the oven. Bake the cake until it springs back when lightly touched and is barely golden in color, 16 to 20 minutes. Cool the cake on a wire rack until it reaches room temperature.

Meanwhile, make the filling by placing the bowl of a stand mixer and its whisk attachment in the freezer for 5 minutes. Fit the cold bowl and whisk to the mixer and whip the $1^1/_2$ cups of cold heavy cream and 1 cup of the cold butterscotch sauce together on medium-low speed until the ingredients are blended. Gradually turn the mixer up to high speed and whip just until the cream holds soft peaks but is not yet stiff.

To cut the cake for assembly, keep the cake in its pan and orient the pan so the longer side is closest to you. Cut the cake with a serrated knife into four equal pieces measuring 4 by 12 inches. Cut through the underlying parchment paper with a pair of scissors in the same places that you cut the cake so you have four quarters of cake (with parchment paper) that can each move independently.

Leaving the cake in the pan, spread a bit more than half of the butterscotch cream evenly over the cake and sprinkle with the toasted almonds. Refrigerate the remainder of the cream while you roll up the cake.

Here comes the fun part: rolling the cake! With the pan still oriented with the longer side closest to you, lift up the nearest edge—both cake and paper—of one of your 4 strips. Using the parchment paper as the cake's support, begin to tuck the cake into a roll and continue tucking (and peeling away the parchment paper) while gently rolling the cake away from you into a roll. Place the rolled cake upright on a serving plate, so that the spiral of cake and filling is visible at the top. (Don't worry, it gets easier from here.) Lift up the next cake strip, using the parchment paper to support it, and wrap the strip around the roll on the serving plate, beginning where the outside edge of the first cake left off, in order to create a bigger roll. Continue with the next two strips, beginning the wrap where the last left off, to make one enormous rolled up cake. Finish by frosting the sides with the remainder of the cream (you might need to give the cream a few turns with a hand whisk to stiffen it up), leaving the top free to show off the spiral of cake and cream. Refrigerate the cake for at least 1 hour and up to 1 day, lightly wrapped in plastic. Just before serving, warm the remaining butterscotch sauce and drizzle it over the individual servings.

Well wrapped and refrigerated, this cake keeps for up to 3 days.

German Chocolate Roll

Contrary to popular belief, German chocolate cake is actually not from Germany at all. It's named after Sam German, an American who developed a brand of sweetened baking chocolate. It was originally called German's Chocolate Cake in the 1950s, but the "s" got dropped along the way, thus giving rise to a false impression of this cake's origin. Don't be shy about rolling the cake in this recipe: it is sturdy and can handle a novice learning how to roll a cake for the first time. Make the ganache before you make the cake, so it has time to set.

10 to 12 servings	bake time	pan
	15 minutes	12 by 16-inch jelly roll pan: grease the pan with spray, then line with parchment paper, then spray the parchment paper as well

FILLING

³/₄ cup heavy cream

¹/₂ cup (3¹/₂ ounces) sugar

2 egg yolks

3 tablespoons (1¹/₂ ounces) unsalted butter, cut into small cubes

1 tablespoon pure vanilla extract

Generous pinch of fine sea salt

¹/₂ cup (2 ounces) toasted chopped pecans (see Toasting Nuts, page 114)

1 cup (4 ounces) lightly packed sweetened shredded coconut

CAKE

6 ounces bittersweet chocolate, chopped or chips

¹/₄ cup brewed coffee (left over from your morning brew is fine)

3 tablespoons (1¹/₂ ounces) unsalted butter, cut into small cubes

6 eggs, separated and at room temperature

¹/₄ teaspoon sea salt

1 teaspoon pure vanilla extract

¹/₂ cup (3¹/₂ ounces) sugar

³/₄ cup Chocolate Ganache (page 146)

To make the filling, whisk together the heavy cream, sugar, and yolks in a small saucepan. Add the butter and place the pan over medium heat, whisking until the filling thickens and just begins to bubble, about 5 minutes. Remove the pan from the heat and strain the custard through a fine mesh sieve into a bowl. Whisk in the vanilla and salt. Place the bowl in the refrigerator to cool while you make the cake, giving the filling a stir every once in a while to encourage the cooling process. Once the filling has cooled, stir in the pecans and coconut, and let stand at room temperature for 15 minutes.

Center an oven rack and preheat the oven to 350°F.

To make the cake, place the chocolate, coffee, and butter in a heat-resistant bowl over a pot of simmering water on medium heat. Stir occasionally until the chocolate is melted and the mixture is smooth. Remove the bowl from the heat and let it cool slightly before whisking in the egg yolks, a couple at a time, blending well between additions, followed by the vanilla.

In the clean bowl of a stand mixer fitted with the clean whisk attachment, combine the egg whites and salt and mix on low speed to combine. Gradually increase the speed to medium-high, whipping until the whites just form soft peaks. With the mixer on medium speed, gradually add the sugar in a slow stream. Kick the mixer up to high speed and continue whipping until the whites just hold firm (not stiff) peaks.

With a rubber spatula, fold one-quarter of the whites into the chocolate batter to lighten it up, then gently fold the chocolate batter into the remaining whites just until combined. Pour the batter into the prepared pan, spreading it out to the edges and smoothing the top. Place the cake in the middle of the oven and bake until the cake springs back when gently pressed, about 15 minutes. Place the cake, still in its pan, on a wire rack until cool.

To assemble the cake, keep the cake in the pan and use a metal spatula to spread the filling over it, leaving $1/4$ inch around the edges. (The layer of filling will be somewhat thin.) Orient the pan so one of the short ends is closest to you. Lift up the edges of both the cake and the parchment paper on this shorter side. Using the parchment paper as the cake's support, begin to tuck the cake into a curve and continue tucking (and peeling away the parchment paper) while gently rolling the cake away from you into a spiral from one short end to the other. Don't worry if the cake cracks a little; you will cover it with ganache. Transfer the cake, seam side down, to a serving platter. Trim off the ends of the roll and frost as desired with the ganache. I like to leave the ends free of ganache so the spiral is visible.

This cake is best served at room temperature and can sit out for up to 4 hours. Well wrapped and refrigerated, the cake keeps for up to 3 days.

Coffee Crunch Spiral

I have taken liberties here with the famous Coffee Crunch Cake from Blum's Bakery in San Francisco. Ernest Weil, the original baker of this delicious cake, developed the recipe in the 1940s. I have turned this classic from a lemon layer cake filled with coffee cream into a chiffon roll, and altered the coffee crunch topping with the addition of finely ground coffee beans. The cake is a cinch to make, so long as you pay attention while you are making the topping, which requires a candy themometer.

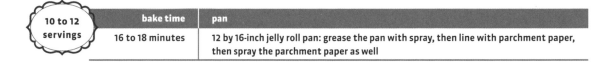

10 to 12 servings	bake time	pan
	16 to 18 minutes	12 by 16-inch jelly roll pan: grease the pan with spray, then line with parchment paper, then spray the parchment paper as well

CRUNCH TOPPING

2 teaspoons baking soda

1 tablespoon finely ground coffee beans

1¹/₂ cups (10¹/₂ ounces) sugar

¹/₄ cup light corn syrup

¹/₄ cup strong brewed coffee

CAKE

1 cup (4 ounces) sifted cake flour

1 teaspoon baking powder

¹/₂ teaspoon fine sea salt

1 cup (7 ounces) sugar

¹/₃ cup canola oil

4 egg yolks, at room temperature

¹/₃ cup water

1 teaspoon pure vanilla extract

6 egg whites, at room temperature

¹/₄ teaspoon cream of tartar

FILLING

1 tablespoon instant espresso powder

2 cups heavy cream

¹/₃ cup (2¹/₃ ounces) sugar

2 tablespoons Kahlua, or
2 teaspoons pure vanilla extract

To make the crunch topping, first generously oil a large baking sheet and set it near your stove. Sift the baking soda into a bowl and whisk in the ground coffee beans. Set this mixture near the stove as well. In a tall and heavy saucepan, combine the sugar, corn syrup, and brewed coffee over medium heat, stirring often, until the sugar has dissolved. Stop stirring and cook the syrup until it reaches 290°F. As the temperature creeps up toward 275°F, give it an occasional stir to prevent the bottom from burning. Once the temperature reaches 290°F, remove the saucepan from the heat and quickly stir in the baking soda and ground coffee. The syrup will foam up wildly, but keep stirring until the baking soda and ground coffee are completely mixed into the syrup. While it is still foaming, pour the syrup onto the greased cookie sheet. Although it is tempting, do not spread it out! Allow the crunch to sit for an hour to firm up. Once it's hard, place the crunch either in an airtight plastic bag or between two pieces of parchment paper. Pound a rolling pin over the bag or paper to crush the crunch into small pieces. The smaller the pieces, the easier they will be to cut and eat later. The crunch can be made up to a week ahead and kept in an airtight container at room temperature.

Center an oven rack and preheat the oven to 325°F.

To make the cake, sift together the flour, baking powder, salt, and ³/₄ cup of the sugar into a large bowl, then whisk to ensure the ingredients are well mixed. In a small bowl, whisk together the oil, yolks, water, and vanilla. Add the liquid mixture to the dry ingredients and briskly stir with a rubber spatula until the mixture is just smooth. Do not overmix.

continued

In the clean bowl of a stand mixer fitted with a clean whisk attachment, whip the egg whites on medium speed until frothy. Add the cream of tartar and gradually increase the speed to high, whipping until the whites just form soft peaks. With the mixer on medium speed, gradually add the remaining $1/4$ cup of sugar. Return the mixer to high speed and continue whipping until the whites just begin to hold firm, shiny peaks. Fold about a third of the whites gently into the batter using as few strokes as possible, then add the remaining whites and fold only until evenly combined.

Pour the batter into the prepared pan, smooth the top, and place the pan in the middle of the oven. Bake the cake until it springs back when gently touched and is lightly golden, 16 to 18 minutes. Cool the cake on a wire rack until it reaches room temperature.

To make the filling, place the bowl and whisk attachment of a stand mixer in the freezer for 5 minutes to chill. Meanwhile, whisk the espresso powder into $1/2$ cup of the heavy cream until dissolved. In the cold bowl of the mixer, whisk all the heavy cream (including the coffee-flavored cream) with your mixer on medium-low, gradually turning up the speed to high. When the whisk begins leaving tracks in the cream, add the sugar in a steady stream and whip just until there are soft—not stiff—peaks. Add the Kahlua or vanilla and whisk until blended.

To assemble the cake, keep the cake in the pan and spread half of the coffee cream evenly over the cake, leaving $1/4$ inch around the edges. Orient the pan so one of the short sides is closest to you. Lift up the edges of the cake and the parchment paper on this shorter side. Using the parchment paper as the cake's support, begin to tuck the cake into a curve and continue tucking (and peeling away the parchment paper) while gently rolling the cake away from you into a spiral from one short end to the other. Don't worry if the cake cracks a little; you will cover it with more coffee cream. Transfer the cake, seam side down, to a serving platter. Trim off the ends of the roll and frost with the other half of the cream. Refrigerate the log for at least one hour or up to 3 days lightly wrapped in plastic wrap in the refrigerator. Just before serving, remove the log from the refrigerator and coat it with coffee crunch.

Well wrapped and refrigerated, the cake (minus the crunch) keeps for up to 3 days. The moisture from the cream will cause the crunch to become chewy, so it's best to eat the whole cake within a few hours after coating it with the crunch topping.

Chocolate Apricot Upside-Down Cake

Fresh apricots are a brief summer delight. I find them at our local farmers' market in July and love to make this cake when they are at their peak. Don't even dream of using dried apricots for this recipe! Instead, substitute pitted sour cherries or fresh cranberries to extend this cake's season.

8 to 10 servings	bake time	pan
	50 minutes	9 by 2-inch round cake pan, sides and bottom greased with 1 tablespoon of soft unsalted butter and bottom lined with a parchment paper circle

TOPPING

¹/₄ cup (2 ounces) unsalted butter

³/₄ cup (5²/₃ ounces) firmly packed brown sugar

6 medium apricots, firm but ripe, washed, pitted, and sliced into quarters

CAKE

4 ounces bittersweet chocolate, chopped or chips

¹/₂ cup (4 ounces) unsalted butter

1 cup (5 ounces) all-purpose flour

³/₄ cup (5¹/₄ ounces) sugar

¹/₄ cup (1 ounce) lightly packed premium unsweetened Dutch-processed cocoa (see Cocoa Confusion, page 35)

1¹/₂ teaspoons ground cardamom

¹/₂ teaspoon baking soda

¹/₂ teaspoon fine sea salt

2 eggs

³/₄ cup buttermilk, at room temperature

2 teaspoons pure vanilla extract

Whipped cream, for serving

Center an oven rack and preheat the oven to 350°F.

To make the topping, melt the butter in a skillet over medium heat. Whisk the sugar into the melted butter until it dissolves. Continue cooking and whisking until the mixture melds together and turns into a caramel darker than its original color. Pour the caramel into the prepared cake pan and set it aside to cool for a few minutes before you arrange the apricot quarters, cut side down, on top of the caramel.

To make the cake, melt the chocolate and butter in a bowl set over a saucepan of simmering water, stirring occasionally until smooth. Remove the bowl and set it aside to cool slightly.

In a large bowl, sift together the flour, sugar, cocoa, cardamom, baking soda, and salt. Whisk the mixture by hand to ensure that the ingredients are well mixed.

Blend the eggs, buttermilk, and vanilla into the chocolate mixture. Add this mixture to the dry ingredients and stir the batter together with a rubber spatula until just combined. Pour the batter on top of the apricots in the pan. Give the pan a few light taps on the counter to help settle the batter.

Place the pan in the middle of the oven and bake until a toothpick inserted into the top half of the cake comes out clean, about 50 minutes. Cool the cake in its pan on a wire rack for 30 minutes and then invert the cake onto a plate, leaving the pan on top of the cake until you are ready to serve it (this conserves heat). Lift the pan off the cake and peel off the parchment paper. Serve warm with a dollop of whipped cream.

This cake is best the day it is made, but any leftovers can be stored in an airtight container (or under a cake dome) at room temperature for up to 2 days.

White Chocolate Rhubarb Downside-Up Cake

The cake showcases rich white chocolate undertones with a tart rhubarb bite. Good rhubarb and high-quality white chocolate are both important for this recipe to shine. Look for white chocolate with a high cocoa butter content, which will taste creamy and rich. Pick bright, sturdy rhubarb stalks that are perky and not bruised.

8 to 10 servings	bake time	pan
	55 to 60 minutes	9 by 2-inch round cake pan, sides and bottom greased with 1 tablespoon of soft unsalted butter, then lined with parchment paper greased with a bit more butter

TOPPING

¾ cup (5¼ ounces) sugar

2 tablespoons water

1 tablespoon lemon juice

2 tablespoons (1 ounce) unsalted butter, cut into cubes

1½ pounds rhubarb, trimmed and cut on a sharp bias into long, thin pieces (about 4 cups or 1 pound when prepped)

To make the topping, place the sugar, water, and lemon juice in a heavy saucepan (one with a tight-fitting lid) and stir until the sugar dissolves. Once dissolved, stop stirring for the rest of the caramelizing process (see page 101). Bring the mixture to a boil over medium heat, then cover and cook for 2 minutes. (Covering in this way allows the steam to wash down the sides of pan, which will prevent any sugar crystals from forming; alternatively, you can keep the lid off and use a clean pastry brush and some water to wash down the sides of the pan.) Uncover the saucepan and continue to boil the sugar, gently and slowly swirling the pan as needed to cook the caramel evenly until it becomes a dark amber color. Carefully add the butter cubes and swirl the pan to melt the butter (the caramel will foam up—be careful!). Pour the caramel into the prepared pan and set it aside to firm up, about 5 minutes. You have two options at this point: for a rustic approach, simply toss the rhubarb into the pan on top of the caramel. For a more refined cake, arrange the fruit in a pattern on top of the syrup (remember, whatever you put face down will be face up when you serve the cake). Once you've added the fruit, set the pan aside.

CAKE

4 ounces premium white chocolate, chopped

$^{1}/_{4}$ cup boiling water

1$^{1}/_{2}$ cups (7$^{1}/_{2}$ ounces) all-purpose flour

$^{3}/_{4}$ cup (5$^{1}/_{4}$ ounces) sugar

2 teaspoons baking powder

1$^{1}/_{2}$ teaspoons ground ginger

1 teaspoon fine sea salt

$^{1}/_{2}$ cup (4 ounces) unsalted butter, at room temperature, cut into small cubes

$^{1}/_{2}$ cup buttermilk, at room temperature

2 eggs

2 teaspoons pure vanilla extract

Strawberry ice cream, for serving (optional)

To make the cake, place the white chocolate in a small bowl and cover with the boiling water. Leave the bowl alone for 2 to 3 minutes, then whisk the now-softened chocolate and set it aside to cool further.

In the bowl of a stand mixer, sift together the flour, sugar, baking powder, ginger, and salt. Using the paddle attachment of your mixer, blend the ingredients together on low speed for 30 seconds. Toss in the cubed butter and the buttermilk and mix on low speed until all the ingredients are moistened, scraping the bowl once or twice to gather all the ingredients. Blend the batter on medium high for 45 seconds. Scrape down the sides and add the eggs, one at a time, on low speed just until incorporated, then blend in the vanilla. Pour in the chocolate and blend on low speed. Scrape down the sides of the bowl and mix on medium high for 45 more seconds. (Don't be alarmed if the batter takes on a curdled appearance at this stage.) Spoon the batter over the rhubarb, covering the caramel and fruit completely. Evenly spread the batter out to the sides of the pan. Place the pan in the middle of the preheated oven and bake until a toothpick inserted into the top half of the cake comes out clean (the cake will turn a dark brown), 55 to 60 minutes. Cool the cake in its pan on a wire rack for 1 hour, and then invert the cake onto a plate, leaving the pan on top of the cake until you are ready to serve it (this conserves heat). When you are ready to serve it, lift off the pan and peel off the parchment paper. This cake is great served just slightly warm with a scoop of strawberry ice cream.

This cake is best the day it is made, but any leftovers can be stored in an airtight container (or under a cake dome) at room temperature for up to a day.

Layer Cakes

The cakes in this chapter are both elegant and easy. Unlike the festively frosted cakes in the next chapter, many of the recipes here stop short of frosting the outside of the cake, leaving the cake layers and the filling exposed to show their flavorful tiers. Stack Cake (page 90) gets a bit carried away with its six layers of cake, held together by a delicious plum compote. Other recipes here call for multiple fillings: Goober Cake (page 111) has both a dreamy peanut butter frosting and a decadent chocolate ganache between its layers, while the layers of Cassata Cake (page 108) house fresh strawberries and a ricotta cream filling. For a unique cake, try the Blitz Torte (page 113), composed of a layer of toasted meringue, dense yellow cake, and a honey custard. And the decadent Red Velvet Cake (page 96), as with many other cakes in this chapter, assembles in a snap: just slather the filling in between the layers and on top, and serve.

These cakes each had their day in the sun during the last century. In the early 1900s, Jam Cake (page 103), Shinny (aka Lane) Cake (page 88), and Cassata Cake were all popular desserts on the American dinner table. By the 1930s, Goober Cake and Carrot Cake (page 94) had gained an audience. Lovelight Chiffon Cake (page 85) was all the rage in the middle of the century, when chiffon cake, dubbed "the first new cake for 100 years," was introduced by Betty Crocker. And finally, by 1976, American households with a wry sense of humor were eating Watergate Cake with Impeachment Frosting (page 99), a cake made with instant pistachio pudding (you won't find that ingredient here).

Lovelight Chocolate Chiffon Cake with Chocolate Whipped Cream

The adjective "lovelight" was inspired by the comments of homemakers who tested Betty Crocker chiffon recipes in the 1950s, as part of a nationwide home recipe testing program. Many of them shared that their husbands loved the delicate and feathery light chiffon cakes—and so the term "lovelight" was coined. With a chocolate whipping cream filling, this chiffon cake is sublime.

8 to 12 servings	bake time	pan
	50 to 55 minutes	10-inch straight-sided metal tube pan or angel food cake pan with feet, ungreased

CHOCOLATE WHIPPING CREAM

8 ounces semisweet chocolate, chopped or chips

3 cups heavy cream

2 teaspoons pure vanilla extract

$1/2$ teaspoon ground cinnamon

$1/8$ teaspoon salt

CAKE

$1/2$ cup (2 ounces) lightly packed premium unsweetened Dutch-processed cocoa (see Cocoa Confusion, page 35)

$1/2$ cup boiling water

$1/2$ cup canola oil

$1/2$ cup buttermilk

2 teaspoons pure vanilla extract

6 egg yolks, at room temperature

$1^3/4$ cups (7 ounces) sifted cake flour

2 teaspoons baking powder

1 teaspoon fine sea salt

$1^1/4$ cups ($9^1/3$ ounces) firmly packed brown sugar

7 egg whites, at room temperature (see Whipping Egg Whites, page 87)

$1/2$ teaspoon cream of tartar

$1/2$ cup ($3^1/2$ ounces) granulated sugar

Begin by making the chocolate whipping cream: place the chocolate in a large heat-resistant bowl. Heat the cream in a saucepan over medium heat until it just comes to a simmer, then quickly remove the pan from the heat and pour the cream over the chocolate. Let the bowl sit for a few minutes so the cream can melt the chocolate, then whisk to blend the cream and chocolate together. Whisk in the vanilla, cinnamon, and salt. Cover with plastic wrap and place in the refrigerator until well chilled, about 3 hours.

Adjust a rack to the bottom third of the oven and preheat the oven to 325°F.

In a small bowl, whisk together the cocoa and boiling water until smooth. Blend in the oil, buttermilk, and vanilla. Whisk in the egg yolks.

In a large mixing bowl, sift together the cake flour, baking powder, and salt. Using a whisk, blend in the brown sugar, working out any large lumps. Stir the chocolate mixture into the dry ingredients with a rubber spatula and briskly stir until the mixture is just smooth. Do not overmix.

In the clean metal bowl of a stand mixer fitted with the clean whisk attachment, whip the egg whites on medium speed until frothy. Add the cream of tartar and gradually increase the speed to medium-high until the whites just hold a soft peak. With the mixer on medium speed, add the granulated sugar in a slow steady stream. Kick the mixer up to high speed and whip until the whites just hold firm, shiny peaks. Fold a third of the whites into the chocolate batter using as few strokes as possible. Add the remaining whites, folding only until evenly incorporated.

continued

Transfer the batter into the pan and bake in the bottom third of the oven until the cake springs back when lightly touched, 50 to 55 minutes. Cool the cake on a wire rack to room temperature (don't invert the cake before it cools, and don't be surprised if it deflates slightly). To unmold the cooled cake, insert a thin knife or metal spatula around the edge of the pan to free the cake from the sides and then invert the cake onto a plate.

To finish the chocolate whipping cream, place the bowl of a stand mixer and its whisk attachment in the freezer for 5 minutes to chill. Place the chocolate cream in the cold bowl and whip until it is thick and spreadable—but don't overwhip it! It's best to err on the underwhipped side, since you can always give it a few strokes with a hand whisk if you need to thicken it up, but if it gets too stiff it can taste grainy (if this happens, see page 41).

To assemble the cake, slice the cake horizontally into thirds. (For guidance, see tips on how to halve a cake on page 10, modifying here for thirds.) Place the bottom third on a serving plate and spread with a third of the cream (about $1^1/_2$ cups). Place the middle layer of cake on top of the cream and spread the next third of the cream over it. Top with the final layer of cake and the remainder of the cream. Chill the cake in the refrigerator for 1 hour before serving.

This cake keeps for up to 2 days in an airtight container in the refrigerator.

Whipping Egg Whites

Properly whipped egg whites are the key to beautiful angel food, chiffon, and sponge cakes, as well as flourless chocolate cakes. Once you get the hang of it, whipping whites becomes second nature. Here's how:

- Don't let any fat infect the whites. Always start with an impeccably clean whisk and bowl (avoid using a plastic bowl, which even when washed can trap fats that will thwart your whipping efforts). Be sure no yolk slips into the bowl.

- Know what result you are aiming for:

    ~ *Soft peaks* are what you have when the whites droop from the tip of the whisk and just begin to hold a faint shape. This is the stage to add the sugar to the whites, if any is called for in the recipe.

    ~ *Medium peaks* hold their shape and are firm but not stiff. They are perfect for chiffon and angel food cakes.

    ~ *Stiff peaks* stand at attention. They should not be dry or appear separated (which means they are overwhipped). They are what you want for Marshmallow Frosting (page 155) or the meringue in Lemon Queen Cakes (page 50).

- Room temperature egg whites whip up best, but it is easiest to separate eggs when they are cold. To warm egg whites to room temperature, nest a bowl of whites in a bowl of warm water and give them a gentle stir.

- Never whip your whites ahead of time. They need to be used immediately after you have whipped them. Once you fold whites into the cake batter, move the cake into the oven in short order.

- Watch your whites at all times. If you are using a mixer, turn it off before the desired stage and finish whipping the whites by hand with a whisk. Overwhipped whites cannot be salvaged.

- Always start mixing your egg whites on low speed until they are frothy, then gradually work up to high speed.

- Egg whites whipped without sugar are more fragile than whites whipped with sugar. Whipping whites with sugar will take a bit longer but be more forgiving. You will achieve stiff peaks, and your end result will be creamier and more stable.

- Egg whites whipped with cream of tartar similarly will be more stable.

Shinny Cake

Now this is my kind of boozy fruit cake! "Shinny" is slang for moonshine. In Harper Lee's novel To Kill a Mockingbird, *Miss Maudie Atkinson is known for her spiked Lane cakes. Scout Finch, the novel's young protagonist, recalled one such cake baked in honor of her Aunt Alexandra coming to live with the Finch family: "Miss Maudie Atkinson baked a Lane cake so loaded with shinny it made me tight"—thus the name of the cake here (though sadly this recipe calls for store-bought bourbon instead of illicitly distilled liquor). My version of Lane cake has a generously boozy custard filling chock-full of dried fruit and chopped nuts, coupled with an irresistibly moist cake. If you want to doll this cake up with frosting, try the meringue frosting found in the recipe for Lemon Queen Cakes (page 50). The original recipe for Lane cake was created by Emma Rylander Lane of Alabama, who first printed the recipe in her 1898 cookbook* Some Good Things to Eat *after she won first prize for the cake at a county fair in Georgia. A tip: chopping the dried fruit into small pieces is easy if you first grease your knife blade.*

10 to 12 servings	bake time	pan
	23 to 25 minutes	Three 8 by 2-inch round cake pans, greased

CREAM CAKE

2¹/₃ cups (9¹/₃ ounces) sifted cake flour

2¹/₄ teaspoons baking powder

1 teaspoon fine sea salt

2 cups heavy cream, cold

1³/₄ cups (12¹/₄ ounces) sugar

4 eggs, at room temperature

2 teaspoons pure vanilla extract

Center an oven rack and preheat the oven to 350°F.

Sift together the flour, baking powder, and salt in a bowl, then whisk the mixture by hand to ensure that the ingredients are well mixed.

Using a stand mixer fitted with the whisk attachment, whip the cream on high speed to soft, droopy peaks. With the mixer on medium-low speed, add the sugar in a steady stream and then return to a high speed to continue to whip the cream until stiff peaks begin to form. Return to a low speed and add the eggs one a time, followed by the vanilla. Stir in the flour mixture in three parts, adding the next addition just as the previous addition is incorporated. Turn off the mixer before all of the flour is completely mixed into the batter and finish mixing the batter by hand.

Pour equal amounts of batter into the three prepared pans (there will be approximately 14 ounces per pan) and bake in the middle of the preheated oven until the cakes are lightly golden and spring back in the middle when gently touched, 23 to 25 minutes. Cool the cakes in their pans on a wire rack for 30 minutes. Gently invert the cakes onto the rack, then flip them right side up and continue to cool on the rack until they reach room temperature.

FILLING

1 cup (7 ounces) sugar

8 egg yolks

³/₄ cup (6 ounces) unsalted butter, cut in small cubes

¹/₂ cup bourbon

¹/₈ teaspoon fine sea salt

2 teaspoons pure vanilla extract

1 cup (4¹/₄ ounces) toasted chopped hazelnuts (see Toasting Nuts, page 114)

1 cup (4 ounces) lightly packed sweetened shredded coconut

¹/₂ cup (3¹/₄ ounces) dried cherries, chopped into small pieces

¹/₂ cup (3¹/₂ ounces) golden raisins, chopped into small pieces

While the cake is cooling, make the filling by whisking the sugar into the egg yolks in a large, heavy-bottomed saucepan. Add the cubed butter and place the pan over medium-low heat, whisking the mixture until the butter melts. Add the bourbon and continue whisking steadily for 3 to 4 minutes, until the mixture begins to simmer and thicken (if you have a thermometer, the mixture should reach 160°F). Remove the pan from the heat and whisk in the salt and vanilla. Pour the mixture into a bowl and refrigerate until cool, giving the filling a stir every once in a while to encourage the cooling process. Once cooled, add the hazelnuts, coconut, cherries, and raisins and let stand at room temperature for 15 minutes.

To assemble the cake, lay one cake on a flat plate with the top side up. Spread the cake with a generous third of the filling. Place the next cake on top of the filling, again top side up. Spread another generous third of the filling here as you did with the bottom layer. Place the third cake on the filling, top side up again, aligning the layers. Slather on the remainder of the filling. Allow the cake to sit for at least an hour to absorb the flavors of the filling.

Cover the cake with a cake dome and store it at cool room temperature for up to 5 days.

Stack Cake

This cake was the traditional wedding cake for settlers in southern Appalachia. Back in the day, wedding guests would each bring one layer of cake, and the bride's family would assemble the layers with a spiced dried apple compote in between—thus the name "stack cake." The more popular the bride (and groom), the taller the cake. What a way to spend your wedding day, making a precariously tall cake! Traditionally, the cake was seasoned with ginger and molasses and baked in a skillet. This six-layer stack cake is baked in cake pans and uses plums or pluots in the filling, not apples. Make the fruit filling first as it needs time to cool off (about 4 hours in the refrigerator) before you can assemble the cake.

12 to 16 servings	bake time	pan
	15 minutes	Three 8-inch round cake pans, greased and bottoms lined with parchment paper circles

FILLING

6 tablespoons (3 ounces) unsalted butter

²/₃ cup (4²/₃ ounces) sugar

2 pounds firm but ripe plums or pluots, washed, pitted, and sliced into ¹/₂-inch slices

¹/₂ vanilla bean, split lengthwise

Pinch of fine sea salt

CAKE

3 cups (15 ounces) all-purpose flour

2 teaspoons baking powder

¹/₂ teaspoon baking soda

1¹/₂ teaspoons ground cinnamon

1 teaspoon ground ginger

¹/₂ teaspoon ground nutmeg

¹/₄ teaspoon ground cloves

1 teaspoon fine sea salt

2 cups (15 ounces) firmly packed dark brown sugar

¹/₂ cup (4 ounces) unsalted butter, at room temperature

¹/₂ cup canola oil

4 eggs, at room temperature

1¹/₂ cups buttermilk, at room temperature

To make the fruit filling, melt the butter in a 12-inch heavyweight sauté pan over medium-high heat. (A large sauté pan is critical because as the plums cook they need to release steam.) Sprinkle the sugar over the melted butter and then carefully distribute the plum wedges evenly across the pan. Toss in the vanilla bean, followed by the salt. Allow the plums to cook, undisturbed, until they begin to release their rosy juices. Try to resist stirring the pan for at least 3 to 4 minutes to encourage a slight caramelizing of the flesh of the fruit. Once the juices begin to come to a steady simmer, turn the heat down to medium and cook the fruit down (you can stir now, and do so frequently!) to the texture of a thick applesauce, about 25 minutes. It is important to cook the fruit long enough to make a thick filling in order to stack a sturdy cake. Fish out the vanilla bean and put the filling, uncovered, in the refrigerator to chill for at least 4 hours, stirring it occasionally to help the cooling process. Your plum filling should yield a generous 2 cups. Made in advance, it can keep for 2 days refrigerated.

Center an oven rack and preheat the oven to 350°F.

Sift together the flour, baking powder, baking soda, cinnamon, ginger, nutmeg, cloves, and salt in a bowl, then whisk the mixture to ensure that the ingredients are well mixed.

In the bowl of a stand mixer fitted with the paddle attachment, blend the brown sugar and the butter together on low speed until the butter has melded into the sugar and the mixture resembles wet sand. As you make

continued

VANILLA GLAZE

1¾ cups (7 ounces) sifted confectioners' sugar

2 tablespoons whole milk

1 tablespoon pure vanilla extract

the batter, stop the mixer frequently and scrape the paddle and the sides of the bowl with a rubber spatula. Still on low speed, drizzle the oil into the mixture. Turn the mixer up to medium-high speed and beat until the batter is fluffy, about 3 minutes. Blend in the eggs one at a time at low speed, adding the next one as soon as the previous one has disappeared into the batter. With the mixer still on low speed, add the flour mixture in three parts, alternating with the buttermilk in two parts, beginning and ending with the flour. After each addition, mix until just barely blended and stop and scrape the bowl. Stop the mixer before the last of the flour has been incorporated and complete the blending by hand with a rubber spatula to ensure you do not overbeat the batter.

Although you will bake only three cakes at a time, you will do this process twice for a total of six cakes. There is no need to refrigerate the batter while it waits its turn. Pour 1 cup (9½ ounces by weight) of batter into each of the prepared pans and bake in the middle of the oven until the centers are just barely firm when lightly touched (the cake will be very blond but have a golden ring around its edge), approximately 15 minutes. Remove the cakes to a wire rack and promptly run a small, thin knife around the edges. Let the cakes cool for 10 minutes before removing them from their pans. Leave the parchment papers on until you assemble the cake. Wipe out the pans with a paper towel, then regrease and repaper them before baking the next three cakes. Once all the layers are baked, be sure to let them all cool to room temperature before assembling the stack.

To assemble the cake, place one of the layers top side up on a flat serving plate. Using a thin metal spatula, spread no more than ⅓ cup of the chilled fruit filling evenly over the layer. Align the next cake layer, again top side up, on top of the previous layer, and repeat with another thin layer of plum filling. Continue with the next four layers of cake and filling, leaving off the filling from the top layer. Whisk together the sifted confectioners' sugar, milk, and vanilla. Pour this glaze over the middle of the cake and allow it to drip down the sides of the stack. Any leftover filling can be refrigerated to spread on your morning toast.

This cake is best served at room temperature. Stored in an airtight container, it keeps for up to 5 days.

Banana Cake with Coffee Walnut Buttercream

Here's a great way to use ripe bananas. You can always mash ripe bananas and freeze them ahead of time. For a more traditional flavor, try Cream Cheese Frosting (page 153).

8 to 12 servings	bake time	pan
	28 to 30 minutes	Three 8 by 2-inch round cake pans, greased and bottoms lined with parchment paper circles

2¹/₂ cups (12¹/₂ ounces) all-purpose flour

1¹/₂ teaspoons baking powder

¹/₂ teaspoon fine sea salt

¹/₄ teaspoon baking soda

1¹/₂ cups mashed ripe bananas (about 3)

³/₄ cup buttermilk, at room temperature

1 cup (8 ounces) unsalted butter, at room temperature

2 cups (14 ounces) sugar

1 tablespoon pure vanilla extract

4 eggs, at room temperature

Coffee Walnut Buttercream (page 149)

Center an oven rack and preheat the oven to 350°F.

In a large bowl, sift together the flour, baking powder, salt, and baking soda, then whisk the ingredients with a hand whisk.

In a small bowl, combine the banana with the buttermilk.

In the bowl of a stand mixer fitted with the paddle attachment, cream the butter, sugar, and vanilla together on high speed until fluffy, about 5 minutes. Stop the mixer frequently and scrape the paddle and the sides of the bowl with a rubber spatula. Blend in the eggs one at a time. With the mixer on low, add the flour mixture in three parts, alternating with the banana mixture in two parts, beginning and ending with the flour. After each addition, and scrape the bowl. Stop the mixer before the last of the flour has been incorporated and complete the blending by hand with a rubber spatula.

Divide the thick batter equally among the prepared pans, and tap the pans on the counter to settle. Bake until the centers spring back when lightly touched, 28 to 30 minutes. Cool the cakes in their pans on a wire rack for 30 minutes. Flip them out and let them continue to cool on the rack, top side up, until they reach room temperature. Leave the parchment paper on until you assemble the cake.

To assemble the cake, lay one of the cakes top side up on a cake plate. Using a metal spatula, frost the top with ³/₄ cup of buttercream out to the edge of the cake (the filling will be about ¹/₄ inch thick). Stack the second cake top side up on top of the frosted cake and spread another ³/₄ cup of buttercream on top of it. Stack the last layer of cake top side up on top. Look for any frosting that may have oozed out the sides and spread it along the

continued

sides of the cake. Apply a thin layer of frosting all over the cake to create a "crumb coat." Place the cake in the refrigerator until the frosting is firm, about 10 minutes. Take it out and frost the cake with the remaining buttercream, using your spatula to make decorative swirls.

Yes, We Have No Bananas

Bananas were considered an exotic treat when they were introduced to the United States at the Philadelphia Centennial Exposition in 1876, where they were wrapped in foil and sold for what was then an extravagant ten cents. Bananas entered the commercial market in the early twentieth century, and soon became quite popular—especially when promoted by the alluring feminine mascot, Chiquita Banana, a creation of the United Fruit Company in the 1940s.

Carrot Cake with Cream Cheese Frosting

Carrot cake originally appeared as a steamed spiced pudding in late 1700s, but carrots apparently fell out of vogue, since recipes for carrot cake weren't published very much (if at all) before the 1930s. Carrot cake then hit mainstream America in the latter half of the twentieth century, gaining popularity in the early 1970s. My twist on this recipe is to add whole wheat pastry flour. I suggest adding walnuts and currants, but in the spirit of the "Me decade" of the 1970s, you can add whatever you want (golden raisins, shredded coconut, pineapple chunks).

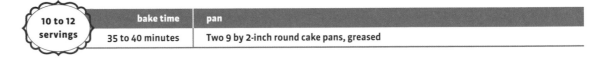

10 to 12 servings	bake time	pan
	35 to 40 minutes	Two 9 by 2-inch round cake pans, greased

1 cup (5 ounces) all-purpose flour

1 cup (4³/₄ ounces) whole wheat pastry flour

1¹/₂ teaspoons baking powder

¹/₂ teaspoon baking soda

¹/₂ teaspoon fine sea salt

1 teaspoon ground cinnamon

1 teaspoon ground ginger

¹/₄ teaspoon ground nutmeg

Center an oven rack and preheat the oven to 350°F.

Sift together the flours, baking powder, soda, salt, ginger, cinnamon, and nutmeg in a bowl, then whisk the mixture by hand to ensure that the ingredients are well mixed.

In the bowl of a stand mixer fitted with the paddle attachment, combine the sugars with the oil on low speed until the mixture resembles wet sand. As you make the batter, stop the mixer frequently and scrape the paddle and the sides of the bowl with a rubber spatula. Add the eggs one at a time,

1½ cups (10½ ounces) granulated sugar

½ cup (3¾ ounces) firmly packed brown sugar

¾ cup canola oil

4 eggs, at room temperature

½ cup buttermilk, at room temperature

1 pound peeled and coarsely grated carrots (approximately 3 cups)

½ cup (2 ounces) chopped walnuts, untoasted

½ cup (2 ounces) dried currants

Cream Cheese Frosting (page 153)

adding the next one as soon as the previous one has disappeared into the batter. Increase the speed to medium-high and blend for 3 minutes. The thick batter will increase in volume and lighten in color. With the mixer on low speed, add the flour mixture in three parts, alternating with the buttermilk in two parts, beginning and ending with the flour. After each addition, mix until just barely blended and stop and scrape the bowl. Stop the mixer before the last of the flour has been incorporated and complete the blending by hand with a rubber spatula to ensure you do not overbeat the batter. Fold in the carrots and walnuts.

Divide the batter evenly into the prepared pans (there will be approximately 1 pound 12 ounces per pan). Divide and sprinkle the currants evenly over the batter. Place the pans in the center of the oven and bake until the cakes are golden and spring back when lightly touched in the middle, 35 to 40 minutes.

Promptly run a knife around the edge of the pan to help the cake retract evenly from the sides.

Cool the cakes in their pans on a wire rack for 30 minutes, and then gently remove the cakes from their pans, taking extra care as they are fragile and could crack. Leave on the parchment paper until you assemble the cake. Continue to cool the cakes on a rack, top side up, until they reach room temperature.

To assemble the cake, place one of the layers, top side up, on a serving plate. Using a metal spatula, spread half of the frosting over the top of the cake, spreading it slightly over the edge of the cake. Place the next layer of cake, top side up again, on top of the frosted layer. Spread the remainder of the frosting over the top of the cake, finishing it in a decorative pattern.

This cake is great the day it is made but can be kept for up to 2 days in an airtight container in the refrigerator (keep it refrigerated due to the frosting). Allow at least 1 hour for the cake to come to room temperature before serving.

Red Velvet Cake with Mascarpone Cream Cheese Frosting

"Velvet" cakes started showing up in the late 1800s, the name referring to any cake with an especially fine crumb. Red velvet cake, meanwhile, grew in popularity in the twentieth century (perhaps because red food coloring, a key ingredient in the cake, became readily available). I scoffed at the thought of garish red velvet cake my whole life up until the making of this book. I'm a northern New England girl who wouldn't ever have thought about putting red food coloring in a cake . . . but WOW, did this cake win me over. It's as beautiful as it is flavorful. I can't imagine that anyone who grew up with a particular red velvet recipe in their heirloom recipe collection will switch from that recipe to mine, but here's one for all those, like me, who didn't grow up with grandma making this cake. Pass it on!

10 to 12 servings	bake time	pan
	28 to 30 minutes	Two 9 by 2-inch round cake pans, greased and bottoms lined with parchment paper circles

2¹/₂ cups (10 ounces) sifted cake flour

¹/₂ cup (2 ounces) lightly packed premium unsweetened Dutch-processed cocoa (see Cocoa Confusion, page 35)

2 teaspoons baking powder

1 teaspoon fine sea salt

³/₄ cup canola oil

2 teaspoons pure vanilla extract

1 tablespoon red food coloring, either gel or liquid (gel color is more intense)

³/₄ cup (6 ounces) unsalted butter, at room temperature

1³/₄ cups (12¹/₄ ounces) sugar

4 eggs, at room temperature

2 egg yolks, at room temperature

1 cup buttermilk, at room temperature

Mascarpone Cream Cheese Frosting (page 152)

Center an oven rack and preheat the oven to 350°F.

In a small bowl, sift together the flour, cocoa, baking powder, and salt, then whisk the ingredients by hand to ensure they are well mixed.

In another small bowl, combine the oil, vanilla, and food coloring.

In the bowl of a stand mixer fitted with the paddle attachment, cream the butter and sugar together on medium-high speed until fluffy, about 5 minutes. As you make the batter, stop the mixer frequently and scrape the paddle and the sides of the bowl with a rubber spatula. With your mixer on low speed, drizzle the oil mixture into the batter until well combined. Turn the mixer gradually up to medium-high speed (avoid splashing the red batter) and beat until fluffy again. Blend in the eggs and egg yolks one at a time, adding the next one as soon as the previous one has disappeared into the batter. With the mixer on low speed, add the flour mixture in three parts, alternating with the buttermilk in two parts, beginning and ending with the flour. After each addition, mix until just barely blended and stop and scrape the bowl. Stop the mixer before the last of the flour has been incorporated and complete the blending by hand with a rubber spatula to ensure you do not overbeat the batter.

Divide the batter evenly into the prepared pans (there will be approximately 1 pound 10 ounces per pan) and smooth the tops. Rap the pans firmly on the counter to release any air bubbles. Place the pans in the middle of the oven and bake until the centers of the cake spring back when lightly touched, 28 to 30 minutes. Cool on a rack for 30 minutes before removing from the pans. Take extra care when removing the cakes from the pans, as they are fragile and could crack. Leave the parchment paper on until you assemble the cake. Continue to cool the cakes on a rack, top side up, until they reach room temperature.

To assemble the cake, place one of the layers, top side up, on a serving plate. Using a metal spatula, spread half of the frosting over the top of the cake, spreading it slightly over the edge of the cake. Place the next layer of cake (top side up again) on top of the frosted layer. Spread the remainder of the frosting over the top of the cake.

This cake is great the day it is made but can be kept for up to 2 days in an airtight container in the refrigerator (keep it refrigerated due to the frosting). Allow at least 1 hour for the cake to come to room temperature before serving.

Watergate Cake with Impeachment Frosting

Ahhh, the early 1970s. I don't know if the era should qualify as "vintage," but it sure was a colorful time in our history, and it gave rise to some popular cakes. Watergate Cake is a pistachio cake with pistachio frosting. It became popular sometime after 1975, the year Kraft Foods developed pistachio pudding mix, and a time when cake mix cakes were at their peak of popularity. Here, I've replicated those flavors from scratch. Using a medium mesh sieve (instead of a fine mesh sieve) to strain the pistachio-infused cream provides some pistachio nut texture in both the pudding and the cake. You can make the caramelized pistachios up to two days in advance; and, if you're not familiar with working with caramel, read the sidebar on page 101 before you begin.

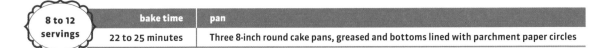

8 to 12 servings	bake time	pan
	22 to 25 minutes	Three 8-inch round cake pans, greased and bottoms lined with parchment paper circles

PISTACHIO PUDDING

1 cup (5 ounces) shelled unsalted pistachio nuts

²/₃ cup (4²/₃ ounces) sugar

1¹/₂ cups half-and-half

4 egg yolks

¹/₂ teaspoon fine sea salt

1 tablespoon cornstarch

CAKE

2 cups (10 ounces) all-purpose flour

1¹/₂ teaspoons baking powder

³/₄ teaspoon fine sea salt

¹/₂ cup (4 ounces) unsalted butter, at room temperature

1¹/₂ cups (10¹/₂ ounces) sugar

¹/₃ cup canola oil

1 tablespoon pure vanilla extract

4 eggs

¹/₂ cup whole milk

Begin by making the pistachio pudding. In the bowl of a food processor fitted with the metal blade, grind the pistachios with ¹/₃ cup of the sugar until finely ground but not a paste. In a medium saucepan over low heat, heat the half-and-half and the ground pistachio mixture until the half-and-half is hot but not boiling. Meanwhile, thoroughly whisk together in a small bowl the egg yolks, the remaining ¹/₃ cup of sugar, and the salt, then whisk in the cornstarch. Slowly whisk about a third of the hot pistachio cream into the yolk mixture. Pour the resulting mixture back into the saucepan with the hot half-and-half and gently cook over medium-low heat, whisking steadily, until the mixture begins to thicken and has been bubbling for roughly 1 minute (you will need to stop whisking for a moment to check if it is bubbling). The mixture will get thick quickly. Strain the mixture through a medium mesh sieve into a shallow bowl or pie pan. Place a piece of plastic wrap directly on the surface of the pudding and refrigerate until cool, about 1 hour. The pudding can be made up to 1 day ahead.

Center an oven rack and preheat the oven to 350°F.

To make the cake, sift together the flour, baking powder, and salt in a bowl and then whisk the ingredients by hand to ensure they are well mixed.

Measure out 1 scant cup of the pistachio pudding and set it aside. In the bowl of a stand mixer fitted with the paddle attachment, blend the butter and sugar together on low speed until the ingredients are well blended. With the mixer on low speed, drizzle the oil and the vanilla into the mixture

continued

PISTACHIO CREAM
(AKA IMPEACHMENT FROSTING)

1 cup heavy cream

1 cup (8 ounces) mascarpone

2 tablespoons sugar

2 teaspoons pure vanilla extract

CARAMELIZED PISTACHIOS

1/4 cup (1 3/4 ounces) sugar

2 tablespoons water

1/3 cup (1 2/3 ounces) shelled unsalted raw pistachio nuts

Small pinch of high-quality sea salt (such as fleur de sel or Maldon)

until combined. Kick up the speed to medium-high and beat until fluffy, about 5 minutes. As you make the batter, stop the mixer frequently and scrape the paddle and the sides of the bowl with a rubber spatula. With the mixer on low speed, blend in the eggs one at a time, adding the next one as soon as the previous one has disappeared into the batter. Add the flour mixture in three parts, alternating with the milk mixture in two parts, beginning and ending with the flour. After each addition, mix until just barely blended and stop and scrape the bowl. Stop the mixer before the last of the flour has been incorporated. Stir in the scant cup of pistachio pudding and complete the blending by hand with a rubber spatula to ensure you do not overbeat the batter.

Divide the batter evenly into the prepared pans (there will be approximately 1 pound per pan) and smooth the tops. Bake in the middle of the oven until the cakes are very lightly golden and spring back when touched, 22 to 25 minutes. Cool the cakes in their pans on a wire rack for 30 minutes. Invert the cakes onto the rack (you will leave on the parchment paper until you assemble the cake) then turn them so they are top side up and continue to cool them on the rack until they reach room temperature.

While the cake is cooling, make the pistachio cream (aka Impeachment Frosting). Place the bowl of a stand mixer and its whisk attachment in the freezer for 5 minutes to chill. Measure out 1 cup of the pistachio pudding into a medium-sized bowl and set it aside. Place the cream, mascarpone, sugar, and vanilla in the cold bowl and mix on low speed until the mixture has come together. Gradually increase the mixer's speed to high and whip until firm peaks just begin to form. It is important to stop beating once the firm peaks form; mascarpone is a fragile cream and tends to become grainy if it is overwhipped. Gently fold one third of the mascarpone cream into the pistachio pudding to lighten it up. Continue gently folding the mascarpone cream into the mixture in thirds until fully combined.

To make the caramelized pistachios, grease a baking sheet lightly with cooking spray and set it aside. Place the sugar and water in a saucepan over medium heat and stir until the sugar dissolves. Bring this syrup to a boil and cook without stirring until it turns light amber in color (you can swirl the pan instead of stirring to distribute the color and the heat). Add the pistachios and swirl to coat the nuts completely in caramel. Continue cooking until the syrup turns a dark amber. Quickly dump the nuts onto the greased baking sheet and lightly dust with salt. Using your hands, clump the nuts into small clusters or separate the individual nuts before the mixture cools, but do this with caution as the sugar holds onto the heat and could burn your fingertips! Cool the nuts and store in an airtight container at room temperature for up to 2 days.

To assemble the cake, remove the parchment from the cake layers. Lay one of the cakes on a serving plate, top side up. Spread a generous cup of pistachio cream over the cake, spreading the filling out and slightly over the edge of the cake. Set the next cake layer (again top side up) on top of the filling and spread another layer of pistachio cream over it like you did with the first. Finish with the top layer of cake (top side up) and spread the remaining pistachio cream over the top surface of the cake.

Garnish the cake with the caramelized pistachios just before serving. (Note that if you refrigerate the caramelized nuts, they will start to weep, the caramel reverting to liquid—so best to put them on the cake just before serving it.)

Due to the pistachio cream, this cake must be refrigerated but it tastes best at room temperature. Pull the cake from the refrigerator at least 1 hour before serving. Place any leftovers in an airtight container in the refrigerator for up to 3 days.

Making Caramel

- Start with clean cane sugar and clean utensils.

- Keep the heat level consistent. Medium-high heat is best.

- Watch the caramel at all times when it's on the stove.

- Use a spoon that won't absorb the heat or melt!

- Don't stir once the caramel comes to a boil; just swirl the pan. If you stir, the caramel is likely to crystallize.

- Use a clean pastry brush dipped in cold water to wash down the sides of the pan. This helps keep the sugar from crystallizing.

- When adding liquid to caramel, always remove the pan from the stove and then add the liquid slowly. The hot caramel will boil up when liquid is added.

- Never forget: the caramel is hot!

Jam Cake with Caramel Chocolate Ganache

Filled with spices, buttermilk, and jam, this moist cake has been in the baking repertoire of my husband's family for over a century. Although this particular recipe hails from Bowling Green, Kentucky, I found many other recipes for jam cake that originated further south. At first glance, I mistakenly thought the jam was merely a filling between the cake layers but to my happy surprise, the jam is actually an ingredient in the batter, creating a lovely berry hue to the cake and an even better berry taste. This down-home cake traditionally calls for a sweet caramel frosting, but I opted for a decadent caramel chocolate ganache. Make the ganache before you make the cake, as it needs about 3 hours to firm up at room temperature (and is so much better when not refrigerated).

12 to 16 servings	bake time	pan
	32 to 34 minutes	Three 8-inch round cake pans, greased and bottoms lined with parchment paper circles

2³/₄ cups (13³/₄ ounces) all-purpose flour

1 teaspoon baking soda

1 teaspoon ground cinnamon

¹/₂ teaspoon ground nutmeg

¹/₄ teaspoon ground cloves

1 teaspoon fine sea salt

1¹/₂ cups (17¹/₄ ounces) jam, preferably blackberry, raspberry, or apricot

³/₄ cup buttermilk, at room temperature

³/₄ cup (6 ounces) unsalted butter, at room temperature

1¹/₂ cups (10¹/₂ ounces) sugar

4 eggs, at room temperature

1 cup (4 ounces) sliced natural almonds, toasted (see Toasting Nuts, page 114)

Caramel Chocolate Ganache (page 147)

Center an oven rack and preheat the oven to 325°F.

In a large bowl, sift together the flour, baking soda, cinnamon, nutmeg, cloves, and salt, then whisk the mixture to ensure that the ingredients are well distributed.

In a small bowl, stir together the jam and the buttermilk.

In the bowl of a stand mixer fitted with the paddle attachment, cream the butter and sugar together on medium-high speed until fluffy, about 5 minutes. As you make the batter, stop the mixer frequently and scrape the paddle and the sides of the bowl with a rubber spatula. Blend in the eggs one at a time, adding the next one as soon as the previous one has disappeared into the batter. With the mixer on low speed, add the flour mixture in three parts, alternating with the buttermilk mixture in two parts, beginning and ending with the flour. After each addition, mix until just barely blended and stop and scrape the bowl. Stop the mixer before the last of the flour has been incorporated and complete the blending by hand with a rubber spatula to ensure you do not overbeat the batter.

Divide the batter evenly into the prepared pans (there will be approximately 1 pound 4 ounces per pan) and smooth the tops. Bake in the middle of the oven until the centers are just barely firm when lightly touched, 32 to 34 minutes. Cool the cakes on a wire rack for 30 minutes before removing them from their pans. Once removed, continue to cool the cakes on the rack,

continued

top side up, until they reach room temperature. Leave the parchment paper on until you assemble the cake.

To assemble the cake, place one of the layers, top side up, on a flat plate or a cake board. Using a thin metal spatula, spread a thin layer of caramel ganache (a bit more than 1/2 cup) on top of the cake and out to the edges of the cake. Sprinkle 2 tablespoons of almonds evenly over the ganache. Align the next cake layer, top side up, on top of the first one, and repeat with another thin layer of ganache and almonds. Place the final layer of cake on top of the cake. Frost the top heavily and the sides lightly with the remainder of the ganache. Lightly press the remaining toasted almonds on the sides of cake.

This cake is best stored and served at room temperature. In an airtight container, it keeps for up to 5 days.

Italian Cream Cake

This cake is no more Italian than French toast is French. This white cake flavored with coconut and pecans originated in the South. Even people who don't like coconut love this cake! Traditionally, it's made with cream cheese frosting, but my twist is to layer this cake up with a chocolate ganache enriched with toasted pecans instead.

8 to 12 servings	bake time	pan
	25 to 30 minutes	Three 8 by 2-inch round cake pans, greased

2 cups (10 ounces) all-purpose flour

³/₄ teaspoon baking soda

¹/₂ teaspoon fine sea salt

1¹/₂ cups (10¹/₂) ounces sugar

¹/₂ cup (4 ounces) unsalted butter, at room temperature

¹/₂ cup canola oil

2 teaspoons pure vanilla extract

4 eggs, at room temperature

1 cup buttermilk, at room temperature

¹/₂ cup heavy cream, cold

1¹/₂ cups (6 ounces) lightly packed sweetened shredded coconut

1 cup (4 ounces) toasted chopped pecans (see Toasting Nuts, page 114)

Chocolate Ganache (page 146)

¹/₄ cup (1 ounce) sifted confectioners' sugar, for dusting (optional)

Center an oven rack and preheat the oven to 350°F.

Sift together the flour, baking soda, and salt in a bowl, then whisk the mixture to ensure that the ingredients are well distributed.

In the bowl of a stand mixer fitted with the paddle attachment, cream the sugar and butter together on medium-high speed until fluffy, about 5 minutes. As you make the batter, stop the mixer frequently and scrape the paddle and the sides of the bowl with a rubber spatula. With your mixer on low speed, drizzle the oil and the vanilla into the mixture until well combined. Blend in the eggs one at a time, adding the next one as soon as the previous one has disappeared into the batter. With the mixer on low speed, add the flour mixture in three parts, alternating with the buttermilk in two parts, beginning and ending with the flour. After each addition, mix until just barely blended and stop and scrape down the bowl. Stop the mixer before the last of the flour has been incorporated and complete the blending by hand with a rubber spatula to ensure you do not overbeat the batter.

In a separate bowl, whisk the heavy cream to soft peaks with a hand whisk. Gently fold the cream into the cake batter, followed by the shredded coconut and ¹/₂ cup of the pecan pieces, reserving the other ¹/₂ cup to blend into the ganache.

Divide the batter evenly among the prepared pans (approximately 1 pound and 3 or 4 ounces per pan) and smooth the tops. Bake until the center springs back when lightly touched, 25 to 30 minutes.

Remove the pans from the oven and promptly run a thin knife around the edges of the pans to help the cake retract evenly from the sides. Cool the cakes in their pans on a wire rack for 30 minutes. Flip the cakes out of the

continued

Italian Cream Cake continued

pans and let them continue to cool on the rack, top side up, until they reach room temperature.

While the cake is cooling, mince the remaining $1/2$ cup of pecans and mix them into the ganache.

To assemble the cake, lay one cake top side up on a flat plate. Spread the cake with a $1/4$-inch-thick layer of ganache (approximately one-third of the ganache), spreading it slightly over the edge of the cake. Place the next layer of cake on top of the ganached layer, again top side up. Spread it with another third of the ganache as you did with the bottom layer. Lay the third layer of cake top side up, align the layers, and slather on the remainder of the ganache.

Just before serving, and only if your cake is firmly planted on the plate (or a cardboard round) and won't slide, carefully tilt the cake ever so slightly and dust the sides of the cake with the confectioners' sugar tapped from a fine mesh sieve, rotating the cake to dust the sides evenly. Serve at room temperature.

Under a cake dome or loosely wrapped, this cake keeps for up to 3 days at cool room temperature.

Cassata Cake

The cassata cake was brought to America at the turn of the twentieth century by Italian immigrants from Sicily who made their home in Ohio. It was made famous by LaPuma Spumoni Bakery in Cleveland. While the roots of this cake are Italian, the flavors in this recipe are truly American. I opted for vanilla chiffon instead of sponge cake, omitted the candied orange and substituted zest, and happily included the tasty chocolate shavings. And don't stop with strawberries—fresh raspberries or blackberries would be equally delicious. Let the season inspire you!

10 to 12 servings	bake time	pan
	15 minutes	Three 9 by 2-inch round cake pans, ungreased, bottoms lined with parchment paper circles

CAKE

1³/₄ cups (7 ounces) sifted cake flour

2 teaspoons baking powder

1 teaspoon fine sea salt

¹/₃ cup (2¹/₂ ounces) firmly packed brown sugar

²/₃ cup (4²/₃ ounces) granulated sugar

5 eggs, separated and at room temperature

¹/₂ cup canola oil

¹/₂ cup buttermilk, at room temperature

1 tablespoon pure vanilla extract

¹/₂ teaspoon cream of tartar

RICOTTA CREAM

15 ounces whole milk ricotta

¹/₂ cup (3¹/₂ ounces) sugar

Zest of 1 orange

1 tablespoon pure vanilla extract

One 2-ounce piece bittersweet chocolate

1 cup heavy cream, cold

Center an oven rack and preheat the oven to 325°F.

To make the cake, sift together the flour, baking powder, salt, brown sugar, and ¹/₃ cup of the granulated sugar in a large mixing bowl. Whisk the mixture by hand to ensure that the ingredients are well mixed. In a small bowl, whisk together the egg yolks, canola oil, buttermilk, and vanilla. Gently but thoroughly stir the yolk mixture into the dry ingredients with a rubber spatula until the batter is just smooth. Do not overmix.

In the clean metal bowl of a stand mixer fitted with a clean whisk attachment, whip the egg whites on medium speed until frothy. Add the cream of tartar and gradually increase the speed to high, whipping until the whites just form soft peaks. With the mixer on medium speed, gradually add the remaining ¹/₃ cup of sugar in a slow steady stream. Kick the mixer back up to high speed and whip until the whites just barely hold firm, shiny peaks. Using a rubber spatula, fold a third of the whites into the batter using as few strokes as possible. Fold in the remaining whites.

Divide the batter evenly into the prepared pans (approximately 10 ounces per pan) and smooth the tops. Bake until the cakes are golden brown and a wooden skewer inserted in the middle comes out with moist crumbs attached, about 15 minutes. Cool the cakes to room temperature in their pans on a wire rack.

To make the ricotta cream, puree the ricotta, sugar, orange zest, and vanilla in a food processor until smooth. Transfer the mixture to a small bowl. Put the chocolate in the freezer for 5 minutes before grating it coarsely with a cheese grater, then fold it into the mixture. Cover with plastic wrap and refrigerate for an hour to thicken up.

MACERATED STRAWBERRIES

2 pints strawberries, sliced (set aside a few of the prettiest for decoration)

3 tablespoons orange liqueur

2 tablespoons sugar

Toss the berries in a bowl with the liqueur and sugar. Lightly mash the berries to release their juices, then set aside the bowl.

To finish the ricotta mixture, whip the heavy cream to soft peaks and fold it into the ricotta mixture until just combined.

To assemble the cake, strain the juice from the macerated berries into a small bowl and set the berries aside. Free the cakes from the sides of their pans with a thin knife or metal spatula. Remove the parchment paper and place one of the cakes, top side up, onto a serving plate. Using a pastry brush, brush the top of the cake with a third of the berry juice. Spread half of the berries onto the cake and top with a third of the ricotta cream. Set the second cake atop the ricotta cream top side up, brush it with half of the remaining juice, and layer it with all of the remaining macerated berries and half of the remaining ricotta cream. Top the cake with the last layer, brush it with the remaining juice, and top it with the last of the ricotta cream. Place the reserved fresh berries artfully on top. Chill the cake for 1 hour before serving.

This cake can be kept in an airtight container in the refrigerator for up to 3 days. Bring to room temperature one hour before serving.

Goober Cake

Anyone from the South will recognize the term "goober" as another name for peanut. This peanut butter cake was one of the recipes I discovered in a box of vintage recipes stored in the attic above Baker & Spice Bakery. Peanut butter started appearing in cakes in the 1930s, once peanut butter found its way into the mainstream. I left the sides of this cake exposed to show off the peanut butter and chocolate filling (and to make the cake a bit less sweet), but you can certainly frost the sides if you prefer—just be sure to make half again as much of the peanut butter frosting recipe. As an alternative to chocolate ganache, try using jam instead for a familiar all-American flavor.

8 to 10 servings	bake time	pan
	28 to 32 minutes	Three 8 by 2-inch round cake pans, greased or three 8 by 8 by 2-inch square pans, greased

3 cups (12 ounces) sifted cake flour

1 tablespoon baking powder

1 teaspoon fine sea salt

1¾ cups (12¾ ounces) firmly packed brown sugar

½ cup (4 ounces) unsalted butter, at room temperature

½ cup canola oil

2 teaspoons pure vanilla extract

½ cup (5 ounces) natural crunchy unsalted peanut butter, at room temperature

4 eggs, at room temperature

1¼ cups whole milk, at room temperature

¾ cup Chocolate Ganache (page 146)

Peanut Butter Frosting (page 154)

Center an oven rack and preheat the oven to 350°F.

Sift together the cake flour, baking powder, and salt in a bowl, then whisk the mixture by hand to ensure that the ingredients are well mixed.

In the bowl of a stand mixer fitted with the paddle attachment, blend the brown sugar and the butter on medium speed until they are a smooth paste. With the mixer on low speed, drizzle the oil and the vanilla into the bowl until combined. Increase the speed to medium-high and cream the mixture until it is fluffy, about 5 minutes. As you make the batter, stop the mixer frequently and scrape the paddle and the sides of the bowl with a rubber spatula. Blend in the peanut butter on low speed. Blend in the eggs one at a time, adding the next one as soon as the previous one has disappeared into the batter. With the mixer on low speed, add the flour mixture in three parts, alternating with the milk in two parts, beginning and ending with the flour. After each addition, mix until just barely blended and stop and scrape the bowl. Stop the mixer before the last of the flour has been incorporated and complete the blending by hand with a rubber spatula to ensure you do not overbeat the batter.

Divide the batter evenly among the prepared pans (there will be approximately 1 pound 2 ounces per pan) and smooth the tops. Bake in the middle of the oven until the cakes are golden and firm and have small cracks forming on top, 28 to 32 minutes.

Remove the cakes from the oven and promptly run a thin knife around the edges of the pans to help the cakes retract evenly from the sides. Cool

continued

the cakes in their pans on a wire rack for 30 minutes. Flip the cakes out of the pans. Let the cakes continue to cool on the rack, top side up, until they reach room temperature.

To assemble the cake, place one cake on a flat plate, top side up. Using about one third of the ganache, spread a thin layer onto the top of the cake. If the ganache is warm, pop the cake in the refrigerator to let the ganache firm up before you proceed. Next, spread a third of the peanut butter frosting—about $3/4$ cup—over the ganache. Place the second cake on top of the frosted cake, also top side up. Cover it with a thin layer of ganache and $3/4$ cup of peanut butter frosting, as you did with the bottom layer. Top with the third cake (top side up), align the layers, and spread ganache and peanut butter frosting on the top layer, using up the remainder of both the ganache and the frosting.

This cake keeps for up to 3 days at cool room temperature.

Blitz Torte

This is a perfect summer birthday cake, made even tastier with the addition of summer berries. A popular German cake, this rustic, rough-and-tumble dessert is composed of layers of meringue and rich yellow cake, with a honey custard to bring it all together. The honey custard can be made days in advance. If you like, you can substitute half a cup of your favorite jam for the honey custard.

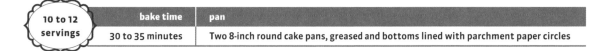

10 to 12 servings	bake time	pan
	30 to 35 minutes	Two 8-inch round cake pans, greased and bottoms lined with parchment paper circles

HONEY CUSTARD

3/4 cup whole milk

2 egg yolks

1/3 cup (4 ounces) honey

1/4 teaspoon fine sea salt

1 1/2 tablespoons cornstarch

2 tablespoons (1 ounce) unsalted butter

CAKE

1 cup (4 ounces) sifted cake flour

1 teaspoon baking powder

1/2 teaspoon ground cinnamon

1/4 teaspoon fine sea salt

1/2 cup (4 ounces) unsalted butter, at room temperature

1/2 cup (3 3/4 ounces) firmly packed brown sugar

4 egg yolks

1 teaspoon pure vanilla extract

3 tablespoons whole milk

First, make the honey custard. Heat the milk over low heat in a small saucepan until hot but not boiling. Meanwhile, thoroughly whisk together in a small bowl the egg yolks, honey, and salt, and then whisk in the cornstarch. Slowly whisk one third of the hot milk into the yolk mixture. Pour this mixture back into the saucepan with the hot milk and gently cook over medium-low heat, whisking steadily, until the mixture begins to thicken and has been bubbling for roughly 1 minute. You will need to stop whisking for a moment to check if it is bubbling. Strain the mixture through a fine mesh sieve into a clean bowl and whisk in the butter until melted. Place a piece of plastic wrap directly on the surface of the custard and refrigerate at least until cool, about 1 hour, or keep in an airtight container in the refrigerator for up to 5 days.

To make the cake, center an oven rack and preheat the oven to 350°F.

In a small bowl, sift together the flour, baking powder, cinnamon, and salt and then whisk the ingredients by hand to ensure they are well mixed.

Using a stand mixer fitted with the paddle attachment, combine the butter and brown sugar together on medium speed until smooth. Add the egg yolks two at a time, blending well between additions. Combine the milk and the vanilla in a separate cup. On low speed, stir in the flour mixture in three additions, alternating with the milk in two additions, beginning and ending with flour mixture. After each addition, mix until just barely blended and stop and scrape the bowl.

Divide the thick batter between the prepared pans (there will be approximately 7 3/4 ounces per pan) and spread it evenly out to the edges of the

continued

TOPPING

¹/₄ teaspoon fine sea salt

4 egg whites

³/₄ cup (5¹/₄ ounces) granulated sugar

1 teaspoon pure vanilla extract

¹/₄ cup (1 ounce) toasted and coarsely chopped hazelnuts (See Toasting Nuts, page 114)

2 teaspoons turbinado sugar

Fresh berries, for serving (optional)

pans. The batter will just barely cover the bottom of each pan. Set the pans aside while you prepare the topping.

To make the topping, put the egg whites and salt into the clean bowl of a stand mixer fitted with the whisk attachment. Whip on low speed until frothy and then add the cream of tartar. Gradually increase the speed to medium-high, whipping until the whites form soft peaks. With the mixer on low speed, slowly add the granulated sugar in a steady stream. Raise the mixer speed again to medium-high and continue whipping until the whites just begin to hold firm, glossy peaks. Fold in the vanilla. Spread even amounts of the meringue on top of the cake batter (approximately 5 ounces per pan) and sprinkle with the hazelnuts and turbinado sugar.

Place the cakes in the middle of the oven and bake until the tops are lightly browned and the cakes have shrunk just slightly away from the sides of the pan, 30 to 35 minutes. Remove the cakes to cool on a wire rack for 20 minutes before removing them from the pans.

To assemble the cake, place one of the cake layers, meringue side up, onto a cake plate. Don't be nervous about the peaks and valleys of the meringue; this is part of the allure of the cake! Spread the honey cream onto the cake. Place the second layer on top, meringue side up. Serve promptly or refrigerate until ready to serve. This cake is great served with fresh berries either on the side, in the middle, on the top, or all of the above.

If you choose to sandwich this cake with jam, it can be kept in an airtight container at room temperature. If filled with the honey cream, it needs to be kept in an airtight refrigerated container. Either way, the cake is best the day it is made but keeps for up to 2 days.

Toasting Nuts

Toasting nuts not only brings out their flavor, it also makes it easier to remove the skins, especially from hazelnuts, one of my favorite ingredients. To toast nuts, spread them evenly out on a baking sheet and place them in a 350°F oven. Alternatively, place them in a heavy skillet over medium-high heat. Either way, give the pan a shake (more frequently if using a skillet) to ensure the nuts don't burn. Once the nuts smell fragrant and begin to brown (about 10 minutes), remove them from the heat. They'll continue to brown a bit as they cool. To remove hazelnut skins, flip the nuts onto a clean kitchen towel and rub them inside the towel as if you were trying to dry them off. Some skins will cling to the nuts, but most will come off.

Party Cakes

For so many festive occasions, it's hard to imagine not celebrating with a cake! Whether we are singing to the birthday girl who is about to blow out her candles or watching a bride and groom take their first sweet bite, the cake is an integral part of the event.

Baking a cake for a special occasion is a loving gesture with a tasty reward that can be shared with all the guests. Although carving out the time to bake, fill, and frost a cake might seem like a daunting task, luckily many components of the cake can be created days before the event. Even a professional cake maker wouldn't dream of making a party cake from start to finish all at once.

First, read through the entire recipe to get an idea of what lies ahead. Map out a plan so you can enjoy the process of making the cake. Feel free to make the cake layers in advance (freezing the unfrosted cake layers doesn't affect the taste), prepare the filling a day or two ahead, make the frosting whenever it's convenient, and then, when you have the time and enthusiasm to assemble the cake, have at it! If you haven't already done so, be sure to read pages 7–13 to learn the ins and outs of making and decorating a layer cake. These tips will help you make and assemble a delicious vintage masterpiece.

Many of the cakes in this chapter are truly timeless. For example, the classic birthday cake combination of chocolate frosting and yellow cake (page 118)—or vice versa, like Black & White Cake (page 123): I might hazard a guess that that cake has been around since the day butter and sugar first met chocolate. Other cakes boomed into their popularity during certain eras, such as Champagne Cake (page 125) and Double Dip Caramel Cake (page 130), both in vogue during the post-war era of the fifties. I've also included more recent flavors from my own childhood, ranging from the taste of Ivins' Famous Spiced Wafers in Gingerbread Icebox Cake (page 138) to the cool York Peppermint Pattie in a flourless chocolate cake (page 142). And I couldn't resist challenging myself with converting back to scratch the Cherry Chip Cake (page 133), so reminiscent of the cake mix cake I adored as a kid.

The Classic

Who hasn't eaten this all-American birthday cake? This recipe is straight out of childhood memory, with no modern twists. The sunny yellow layers, surrounded by rich fudge frosting, will sweeten any birthday. If you plan to frost this cake the same day you bake it, make the frosting while the cake is baking. It will take about an hour from start to finish for the frosting to reach the right consistency, and your timing will be perfect.

8 to 12 servings	bake time	pan
	35 to 40 minutes	Two 8 by 2-inch round cake pans, greased and bottoms lined with parchment paper circles

1¹/₃ cups (5¹/₃ ounces) sifted cake flour

³/₄ cup plus 2 tablespoons (4 ounces) all-purpose flour

1¹/₂ teaspoons baking powder

1 teaspoon fine sea salt

6 tablespoons (3 ounces) unsalted butter, at room temperature

2 cups (14 ounces) sugar

¹/₂ cup canola oil

1 tablespoon pure vanilla extract

4 egg yolks, at room temperature

3 eggs, at room temperature

¹/₂ cup buttermilk, at room temperature

¹/₂ cup heavy cream, cold

Fudge Frosting (page 151)

Center an oven rack and preheat the oven to 350°F. Place a medium bowl in the refrigerator to chill.

Sift together the flours, baking powder, and salt in a bowl, then whisk the mixture by hand to ensure that the ingredients are well mixed.

In the bowl of a stand mixer fitted with the paddle attachment, cream the butter and sugar together on medium-high speed until fluffy, about 5 minutes. As you make the batter, stop the mixer frequently and scrape the paddle and the sides of the bowl with a rubber spatula. With your mixer on low speed, drizzle the oil and the vanilla into the mixture until well combined. Blend in the egg yolks and whole eggs one at a time, adding the next one as soon as the previous one has disappeared into the batter. With the mixer on low speed, add the flour mixture in three parts, alternating with the buttermilk in two parts, beginning and ending with the flour. After each addition, mix until just barely blended and stop and scrape the bowl. Stop the mixer before the last of the flour has been incorporated and complete the blending by hand with a rubber spatula to ensure you do not overbeat the batter.

In a separate chilled bowl, whisk the heavy cream to soft peaks with a hand whisk. Fold the cream into the cake batter. Divide the batter evenly between your two pans (there will be approximately 1 pound 6 ounces per pan) and smooth the tops. Tap the pans lightly on the counter to knock out any large air bubbles.

Bake in the middle of the oven until the cakes crack a bit on top and the centers spring back when lightly touched, 35 to 40 minutes. Cool the cakes in their pans on a wire rack for 30 minutes. Flip the cakes out of the pans, leaving on the parchment paper until you assemble the cake.

Let them continue to cool on the rack, top side up, until they reach room temperature.

To assemble the cake, cut each cake layer in equal halves to create four layers (for tips on halving a cake, see page 10). Lay one of the two bottom layers of cake (cut side up) on a flat plate. Using a metal spatula, frost the top with a heaping $1/2$ cup of frosting, spreading it out to the edge of the cake. Stack the second bottom cake layer cut side up on top of the frosted cake and spread another heaping $1/2$ cup of frosting on top of the cake. Next, align one of the top two layers, cut side up, on top of the frosted cake and repeat with another heaping $1/2$ cup of frosting. Stack the last layer, cut side *down* this time, on top. Look for any frosting that may have oozed out between the layers and spread it along the sides of the cake. Apply a thin layer of frosting all over the cake to create a "crumb coat." Place the cake in the refrigerator until the frosting is firm, about 10 minutes. Take it out and frost the cake with the remaining frosting, using your spatula to make decorative swirls (for additional guidance on how to frost a cake, see page 10).

In an airtight container at room temperature, this cake keeps for up to 3 days.

The Pink Cake

This is a Baker & Spice original, and it's our most popular cake—loved by men and women alike! The buttercream frosting is tinted pink by a raspberry puree (not food coloring)—be sure to save your extra whites from baking the cake to make the frosting. The cake itself is a rich, moist chocolate cake. If you want a go-to recipe for all your choco-late cake cravings, this is the one.

8 to 12 servings	bake time	pan
	22 to 25 minutes	Three 8 by 2-inch round cake pans, greased and bottoms lined with greased parchment paper circles

4 ounces unsweetened chocolate, chopped

¹/₄ cup (1 ounce) lightly packed premium unsweetened Dutch-processed cocoa (see Cocoa Confusion, page 35)

³/₄ cup boiling water

³/₄ cup (6³/₄ ounces) full-fat sour cream

1 tablespoon pure vanilla extract

2 cups (10 ounces) all-purpose flour

³/₄ teaspoon baking soda

1 teaspoon fine sea salt

¹/₂ cup (4 ounces) unsalted butter, at room temperature

1 cup (7¹/₂ ounces) firmly packed light brown sugar

³/₄ cup (5¹/₄ ounces) granulated sugar

¹/₂ cup canola oil

3 egg yolks, at room temperature

3 eggs, at room temperature

Raspberry Buttercream (page 149)

Center an oven rack and preheat the oven to 350°F.

Put the unsweetened chocolate and the cocoa into a small bowl. Pour the boiling water over the chocolate and allow it to steep for 1 minute. Whisk the mixture together. Whisk in the sour cream and vanilla. Set aside.

Sift together the flour, baking soda, and salt in a bowl, then whisk the mixture by hand to ensure that the ingredients are well mixed.

In the bowl of a stand mixer fitted with the paddle attachment, cream the butter and both sugars together on medium-high speed until light, about 3 minutes. As you make the batter, stop the mixer frequently and scrape the paddle and the sides of the bowl with a rubber spatula. On low speed, drizzle the oil into the mixture until blended. Turn the mixer up to medium-high speed and beat until the batter is fluffy, about 3 more minutes. Blend in the eggs and egg yolks one at a time, adding the next one as soon as the previous one has disappeared into the batter. With the mixer on low speed, add the flour mixture in three parts, alternating with the chocolate mix-ture in two parts, beginning and ending with the flour. After each addition, mix until just barely blended and stop and scrape the bowl. Stop the mixer before the last of the flour has been incorporated and complete the blending by hand with a rubber spatula to ensure you do not overbeat the batter.

Divide the thick batter equally among the prepared pans (there will be approximately 1 pound 2 ounces per pan). Smooth the tops and tap the pans on the counter to settle the batter and eliminate any large air bubbles. Bake in the middle of the oven until the centers spring back when lightly touched, 22 to 25 minutes. Cool the cakes in their pans on a wire rack for 30 minutes. Flip the cakes out of the pans, leaving on the parchment paper

continued

until you assemble the cake. Let them continue to cool on the rack, top sides up, until they reach room temperature.

To assemble the cake, lay one of the cakes top side up on a cake plate. Using a metal spatula, frost the top with $3/4$ cup of buttercream, spreading it out to the edge of the cake (the filling will be about $1/4$ inch thick). Stack the second cake top side up on top of the frosted cake and spread another $3/4$ cup of buttercream on top of it. Stack the last layer of cake top side up on top. Look for any frosting that may have oozed out beween the layers and spread it along the sides of the cake. Apply a thin layer of frosting all over the cake to create a "crumb coat." Place the cake in the refrigerator until the frosting is firm, about 10 minutes. Take it out and frost the cake with the remaining buttercream, using your spatula to make decorative swirls (for additional guidance on how to frost a cake, see page 10).

Store the cake in an airtight container at room temperature for up to 3 days.

Sugar Syrup to the Rescue

At Baker & Spice Bakery, before frosting a cake we coat the layers with sugar syrup, which helps to keep the cake moist and adds flavor at the same time. This trick will also help to salvage a dry cake. To make a sugar syrup, combine $1/2$ cup boiling water, $1/4$ cup sugar, and 1 teaspoon pure vanilla extract or other flavoring (such as Kahlua or Grand Marnier) and stir until dissolved. Let the syrup cool, then brush a coat of it onto the top of each cake layer before you frost it.

Black & White Cake

This timeless cake is the reverse of the classic white cake with chocolate frosting: two thick layers of the darkest chocolate cake, slathered with bittersweet ganache and then covered with vanilla bean buttercream. The moist, dense cake tastes even richer and better a day after it is made, so feel free to prepare this ahead. Seek out Hershey's Special Dark Cocoa to produce the darkest chocolate cake imaginable.

8 servings	bake time	pan
	35 to 40 minutes	Two 8 by 2-inch round cake pans, greased and bottoms lined with parchment paper circles

$^3/_4$ cup ($2^1/_4$ ounces) lightly packed Hershey's Special Dark Cocoa or 3 ounces premium unsweetened Dutch-processed cocoa (see Cocoa Confusion, page 35)

$^2/_3$ cup hot coffee (rewarmed from the leftover morning brew works fine)

$^1/_2$ cup ($4^1/_2$ ounces) full-fat sour cream

1 tablespoon pure vanilla extract

$1^1/_2$ cups ($7^1/_2$ ounces) all-purpose flour

$^3/_4$ teaspoon baking soda

$^1/_2$ teaspoon fine sea salt

10 tablespoons (5 ounces) unsalted butter, at room temperature

$1^1/_4$ cup ($9^1/_3$ ounces) firmly packed dark brown sugar

$^1/_3$ cup ($2^1/_3$ ounces) granulated sugar

2 egg yolks, at room temperature

2 eggs, at room temperature

Chocolate Ganache, made with bittersweet chocolate (page 146)

Vanilla Bean Buttercream (page 149)

Center an oven rack and preheat the oven to 350°F.

In a small bowl, whisk together the cocoa and the hot coffee. Blend in the sour cream and vanilla, and set aside.

In another bowl, sift together the flour, baking soda, and salt, then whisk the mixture by hand to ensure that the ingredients are well mixed.

In the bowl of a stand mixer fitted with the paddle attachment, cream the butter and sugars together on medium-high speed until fluffy, about 5 minutes. As you make the batter, stop the mixer frequently and scrape the paddle and the sides of the bowl with a rubber spatula. Blend in the egg yolks and the eggs one at a time, adding the next one as soon as the previous one has disappeared into the batter. With the mixer on low speed, add the flour mixture in three parts, alternating with the cocoa mixture in two parts, beginning and ending with the flour. After each addition, mix until just barely blended and stop and scrape the bowl. Stop the mixer before the last of the flour has been incorporated and complete the blending by hand with a rubber spatula to ensure you do not overbeat the batter.

Divide the thick batter evenly between the two prepared pans (there will be approximately 1 pound 4 ounces per pan) and smooth the tops. Tap the pans on the counter to eliminate any air bubbles. Bake in the middle of the oven until the centers spring back when lightly touched and small cracks have formed on the surface, 35 to 40 minutes. Cool the cakes in their pans on a wire rack for 30 minutes. Flip the cakes out of the pans, leaving on the parchment paper until you assemble the cake. Let them continue to cool on the rack, top sides up, until they reach room temperature.

continued

To assemble the cake, lay one of the cakes top side up on a serving plate. Using a metal spatula, frost the top with $^1/_2$ cup of ganache, spreading it to just shy of the cake's edge. Place the cake in the refrigerator for 5 minutes to firm up the ganache. Take it out and spread 1 cup of the buttercream on top of the ganached cake, taking it to the edge of the cake (you'll completely cover the ganache). Align the second cake, top side up, on top of the buttercream and top the it with another $^1/_2$ cup of ganache, spreading it nearly to the edge and chilling it for 5 minutes to firm up. Look for any buttercream that may have oozed out between the layers and spread it along the sides of the cake. Apply a thin layer of buttercream all over the cake to create a "crumb coat." Place the cake in the refrigerator until the frosting is firm, about 10 minutes. Take it out and finish the cake by frosting it with the remaining buttercream and decorating the top of the cake with ganache "kisses" (for additional guidance on how to frost a cake, see page 10).

Store the cake in an airtight container at room temperature for up to 3 days.

Champagne Cake

When we opened Baker & Spice Bakery, we kept the same phone number as the previous bakery that had inhabited the space for fifty years. Customers from the previous shop kept calling us, asking for "pink champagne cake." Having never heard of such a cake, but loving the bubbles of Champagne, I was determined to find out more about this specialty. To my horror, I learned that the cake was really a white cake made with sherry custard and white frosting tinted pink with red food coloring, and it had no Champagne in it at all! I also discovered that pink champagne cake was all the rage in the 1950s. Here is an updated version—this one full of sparkling wine, in both the cake and the custard. I prefer to leave the whole cake white, as it looks perfectly elegant for a shower or a wedding; it would be wonderful paired with fresh berries. Feel free to add a drop of red food coloring to the frosting and the cake batter. Save your money and go for an inexpensive dry sparkling wine for this recipe.

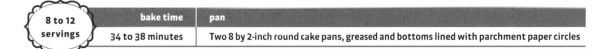

8 to 12 servings	bake time	pan
	34 to 38 minutes	Two 8 by 2-inch round cake pans, greased and bottoms lined with parchment paper circles

CAKE

3 cups (11¼ ounces) sifted cake flour

2½ teaspoons baking powder

½ teaspoon fine sea salt

4 eggs, at room temperature

1¾ cups (12¼ ounces) sugar

2 teaspoons pure vanilla extract

1 cup canola oil

1 cup dry sparkling white wine

CUSTARD

1½ cups half-and-half

4 egg yolks

½ cup (3½ ounces) sugar

Pinch of fine sea salt

⅓ cup dry sparkling white wine

2½ tablespoons cornstarch

2 tablespoons (1 ounce) unsalted butter

1 tablespoon pure vanilla extract

FROSTING

1½ cups heavy cream, cold

3 tablespoons sugar

Center an oven rack and preheat the oven to 350°F.

Sift together the flour, baking powder, and salt in a small bowl, then whisk the mixture by hand to ensure the ingredients are well mixed.

In the bowl of a stand mixer fitted with the paddle attachment, blend the eggs, sugar, and vanilla together on medium speed for one minute. With your mixer on low speed, drizzle the oil into the mixture until well combined. Add the flour mixture in three parts, alternating with the wine in two parts, beginning and ending with the flour. After each addition, mix until just barely blended and stop and scrape the bowl. The batter will be thin. Stop the mixer before the last of the flour has been incorporated and complete the blending by hand with a rubber spatula to ensure you do not overbeat the batter.

Divide the batter evenly between pans (there will be approximately 1 pound and 7 or 8 ounces per pan). Bake in the middle of the oven until the center springs back when lightly touched, 34 to 38 minutes. The cakes will be slightly domed and golden in the center. Cool the cakes in their pans on a wire rack for 30 minutes. Flip the cakes out of the pans, leaving on the parchment paper until you assemble the cake. Let them continue to cool on the rack, top sides up, until they reach room temperature.

continued

To make the custard, heat the half-and-half over low heat in a medium saucepan until it is hot but not boiling. Meanwhile, thoroughly whisk together the egg yolks, sugar, and salt in a bowl. Blend in the wine, followed by the cornstarch. Slowly whisk about a third of the hot half-and-half into the yolk mixture. Pour this mixture back into the saucepan with the remaining hot half-and-half and gently cook over medium-low heat, whisking steadily, until the mixture begins to thicken and has bubbled for roughly 1 minute (you will need to stop whisking for a moment to check if it is bubbling). Strain the mixture through a sieve into a clean shallow bowl and whisk in the butter and vanilla until the butter melts. Place a piece of plastic wrap directly on the surface of the custard and refrigerate until cool, about 1 hour. (The custard can be made up to 2 days ahead.)

Before you begin to assemble the cake, place the bowl and the whisk attachment of a stand mixer in the freezer.

Cut each cake layer in equal halves to create four layers (see page 10). Lay one of the two bottom layers, cut side up, on a flat plate. Using a metal spatula, spread a heaping $1/2$ cup of the custard over the cake layer, out to $1/4$ inch from the edge. Stack the second bottom cake layer, cut side up, on top of the custard layer and repeat with another heaping $1/2$ cup of the custard. Next stack one of the two top layers, cut side up, on top of the new custard layer and repeat with another heaping $1/2$ cup of the custard. You should have about $1/2$ cup of custard left; this will be used in the whipped cream frosting. Stack the last layer of cake, cut side *down* this time, on top of the top custard layer. Check for any custard that may have oozed out between the layers, and spread it along the sides. Refrigerate the cake for 30 minutes or until the cake and custard seem stable.

To make the whipped cream frosting, remove the bowl and whisk attachment from the freezer, pour in the cream, and begin to whip it on medium-low speed. When the whisk begins leaving tracks in the cream, add the sugar. Increase the speed to medium-high and whip until the cream holds a medium-firm peak. Stop the mixer at this point rather than overwhipping the cream, as you can always continue with a few strokes of a hand whisk if you realize the cream is too soft. Fold in the reserved $1/2$ cup of custard. Finish the cake by frosting the sides and top with the whipped cream frosting. Refrigerate the cake for at least 30 minutes to let it set.

Store the cake in an airtight container in the refrigerator for up to 3 days.

Old Vermont Burnt Sugar Cake with Maple Cream Cheese Frosting

Before the days of vanilla and almond extracts, bakers would use a burnt sugar syrup to impart flavor. This moist, delicate cake has that caramel essence. It would be good frosted with chocolate ganache or coffee buttercream, but as a native Vermonter I was compelled to match it with a maple frosting. Try to use grade B maple syrup, which has lovely caramel undertones.

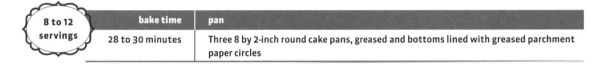

8 to 12 servings	bake time	pan
	28 to 30 minutes	Three 8 by 2-inch round cake pans, greased and bottoms lined with greased parchment paper circles

BURNT SUGAR SYRUP

¹/₂ cup (3¹/₂ ounces) sugar

¹/₂ cup hot water

CAKE

2¹/₂ cups (12¹/₂ ounces) all-purpose flour

2 teaspoons baking powder

¹/₂ teaspoon fine sea salt

³/₄ cup (6 ounces) unsalted butter, at room temperature

1³/₄ cup (12¹/₄ ounces) sugar

¹/₃ cup maple syrup

¹/₃ cup canola oil

1 teaspoon pure vanilla extract

2 egg yolks

4 eggs

1 cup whole milk, at room temperature

Maple Cream Cheese Frosting (page 153)

Center an oven rack and preheat the oven to 350°F.

To make the burnt sugar syrup, place the sugar in a small saucepan or sauté pan that is very clean. Over medium heat, swirl the pan gently to dissolve the sugar; avoid the temptation of stirring, and simply continue swirling the pan until the sugar has melted and is amber in color. It will smoke but don't worry—this is why they call it *burnt* sugar. Remove the pan from the heat and add the hot water, a few drops at a time, being careful when the sugar spatters. Once all the water has been added, put the pan back over medium heat and cook for an additional 5 minutes to reduce the syrup, occasionally stirring with a wooden spoon to incorporate any sugar that is stuck to the bottom of the pan. Remove the syrup from the heat and allow it to cool for 10 minutes.

To make the cake, sift together the flour, baking powder, and salt in a small bowl, then whisk the mixture by hand to ensure that the ingredients are well mixed.

In the bowl of a stand mixer fitted with the paddle attachment, cream the butter, sugar, and maple syrup on medium-high speed until fluffy, about 5 minutes. As you make the batter, stop the mixer frequently and scrape the paddle and the sides of the bowl with a rubber spatula. With your mixer on low speed, drizzle the oil and the vanilla into the mixture until well combined. Blend in the egg yolks and the eggs one at a time, adding the next one as soon as the previous one has disappeared into the

continued

batter. In a small bowl, combine the milk and the burnt sugar syrup. With the mixer on low speed, add the flour mixture in three parts, alternating with the milk-syrup mixture in two parts, beginning and ending with the flour. After each addition, mix until just barely blended and stop and scrape the bowl. Stop the mixer before the last of the flour has been incorporated and complete the blending by hand with a rubber spatula.

Divide the batter evenly among the prepared pans (approximately 1 pound 3 ounces per pan) and smooth the tops. Bake until the cakes are golden and the centers spring back when lightly touched, 28 to 30 minutes. Right after you remove the cakes from the oven, run a thin knife around the edges of the cakes; the cakes will naturally shrink back from the sides of the pan as they cool, and this step ensures they will shrink evenly. Cool the cakes in their pans on a wire rack for 30 minutes. Flip the cakes out of the pans, leaving on the parchment paper until you assemble the cake. Let them continue to cool on the rack to room temperature, top sides up.

To assemble the cake, lay one of the cakes top side up on a flat plate. Using a metal spatula, frost the top with $3/4$ cup of cream cheese frosting, spreading it out to the edge of the cake. Stack the second cake top side up on top of the frosted cake and spread another $3/4$ cup of frosting on top of the cake. Stack the last layer of cake, also top side up, on top. Apply a thin layer of frosting all over the cake to create a "crumb coat." Place the cake in the refrigerator until the frosting is firm, about 15 minutes. Take it out and frost the cake with the remaining frosting (for additional guidance on how to frost a cake, see page 10).

The cake should be served at room temperature. It keeps for up to 4 days stored in the refrigerator in an airtight container. Take it out of the refrigerator at least 1 hour before serving.

Double Dip Caramel Cake

This is a rich cake—cut it in small slices! I found the recipe for double dip caramel cake among the vintage recipes stashed in the attic above Baker & Spice. My twist on the original recipe is to slather the cake with a homemade caramel sauce before frosting it with a sinful caramel frosting. The recipe has a few steps, but each one is worth it for the final decadent result. This cake works best if you first prepare the caramel sauce, then make the cake, and finish up with the frosting.

12 to 16 servings	bake time	pan
	25 to 30 minutes	Three 8 by 2-inch round cake pans, greased and bottoms lined with parchment paper circles

CARAMEL SAUCE

1/4 cup water

1 1/2 cups (10 1/2 ounces) sugar

1 1/2 cups heavy cream

2 teaspoons pure vanilla extract

1 teaspoon fine sea salt

CAKE

4 eggs, at room temperature

2 egg yolks, at room temperature

1 1/2 cups (13 1/2 ounces) full-fat sour cream, at room temperature

1 tablespoon pure vanilla extract

3 cups (12 ounces) sifted cake flour

2 cups (14 ounces) sugar

2 teaspoons baking powder

3/4 teaspoon baking soda

1 teaspoon fine sea salt

3/4 cup (6 ounces) unsalted butter, at room temperature, cut into small cubes

FROSTING

6 cups (1 1/2 pounds) sifted confectioners' sugar

1 1/2 cups (12 ounces) unsalted butter, at room temperature

1/4 cup heavy cream

Center an oven rack and preheat the oven to 325°F.

To make the caramel sauce, gently stir together the water and sugar in a heavy saucepan over medium-high heat, being careful not to splash the sides of the pot. Stop stirring and allow the sugar to boil until it is a rich amber color. To check the true color of the caramel (because it will appear much darker than it actually is), simply tilt the pot to see a thin layer of the liquid—resist the urge to stir or stick an implement into the caramel, as it may cause the caramel to crystallize. Remove the saucepan from the heat and slowly pour in 3/4 cup of the cream, being careful not to burn yourself when the caramel spatters with the addition of the cream. Once the spattering subsides, pour in the remaining 3/4 cup of cream and place the saucepan back on the stove over medium heat, stirring until combined. Remove the pan from the heat and stir in the vanilla and salt. Reserve 1 cup of the caramel for your frosting; the rest will be used to assemble the cake. Place all of the caramel in the refrigerator to cool while the cake bakes.

To make the cake, whisk together the eggs, egg yolks, 1/2 cup of the sour cream, and the vanilla in a small bowl; set aside. In the bowl of a stand mixer fitted with the paddle attachment, blend the flour, sugar, baking powder, baking soda, and salt for 1 minute at low speed. Add the butter and the remaining 1 cup of sour cream and blend on low speed until the batter comes together. This will take some coaxing—you will need to stop the mixer often to scrape the batter from the paddle and the bottom of the bowl. Once the mixture has come together, mix on medium-high speed for an additional 90 seconds. The batter will be thick. Add the egg mixture in thirds, mixing each third into the batter until just combined and scraping the bowl as necessary.

Divide the batter equally among the three prepared pans (there will be approximately 1 pound 2 ounces per pan) and smooth the tops. Bake in the middle of the oven until the centers spring back when lightly touched and a toothpick inserted in the middle comes out just barely moist, 25 to 30 minutes. Cool the cakes in their pans on a wire rack for 30 minutes. Flip the cakes out and lay them on a wire rack, top side up, to cool to room temperature. Leave the parchment paper on until you assemble the cake.

Because the frosting is at its best when fresh, make it just before assembling the cake. In the bowl of a stand mixer fitted with the paddle attachment, cream together the confectioners' sugar and butter on high speed until the mixture is thick, fluffy, and light in color, about 2 minutes. Gradually add the reserved cooled cup of caramel and mix on medium speed until combined. Switch to the whisk attachment and, with the mixer running on low speed, drizzle in the ¹/₄ cup of cream. Turn up the mixer to high speed for 1 to 2 minutes or until the frosting is fluffy.

To assemble the cake, first give the caramel sauce a good stir. If any of the cake layers are domed, slice off the domes. (They are great to nibble on while you're building the cake!) Remove the parchment paper circles. Cut each cake layer in half to yield six thin layers (for tips on halving a cake, see page 10). Build this cake using the three bottom layers first, so that the three top layers constitute the top half of the cake. Place one of the bottom layers cut side up on a serving plate. Using a metal spatula, spread a very thin layer of the caramel (2 to 3 tablespoons) over the cake, then spread a thin layer (¹/₂ cup) of the frosting over the caramel. Don't worry if some of the caramel blends into the frosting, as this just makes it all yummier. Repeat these steps with the two remaining bottom layers, followed by two top layers (all top side up), spreading each layer with caramel first, and then with frosting. Place the very top layer top side down on the cake. Apply a thin layer of frosting all over the cake to make a "crumb coat." Place the cake in the refrigerator for 10 minutes to firm up. Take it out and frost with the remaining frosting (for additional guidance on how to frost a cake, see page 10).

The cake will stay fresh for up to 4 days under a cake dome at room temperature—if it lasts that long!

Cherry Chip Cake with Cherry Buttercream

Cherries and chocolate: the perfect combo! This cake stands tall with three fluffy layers of cake held together by dense bittersweet chocolate ganache and cherry buttercream. Anyone unfamiliar with this cake might expect to taste chocolate chips based on its name, but the chips are actually pieces of cherry in the cake. Cherry chip cake was originally a cake made from scratch with maraschino cherries; then in 1967 Betty Crocker came out with a cherry chip cake mix that was devoured by kids like me. Coming full circle, I wanted to make a cake from scratch that tasted just like my childhood memory, but I did not want to use artificially flavored cherries. After lots of trial and error, I found that dried sour cherries do the trick.

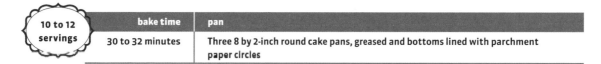

10 to 12 servings	bake time	pan
	30 to 32 minutes	Three 8 by 2-inch round cake pans, greased and bottoms lined with parchment paper circles

CHERRY PUREE

6 ounces dried tart or sour cherries (1 heaping cup)

¹/₄ cup water

1 tablespoon pure vanilla extract

1¹/₄ cups whole milk, at room temperature

CAKE

3 cups (12 ounces) sifted cake flour

2 teaspoons baking powder

¹/₂ teaspoon fine sea salt

¹/₄ teaspoon baking soda

³/₄ cup (6 ounces) unsalted butter, at room temperature

1³/₄ cups (12¹/₄ ounces) sugar

¹/₃ cup canola oil

6 egg whites, at room temperature

Cherry Buttercream (page 148)

³/₄ cup Chocolate Ganache, made with bittersweet chocolate (page 146)

Center an oven rack and preheat the oven to 350°F.

To make the cherry puree, combine the cherries and water in a small saucepan over medium heat. Bring to a simmer and cook until almost all of the water is evaporated and the cherries have plumped up, about 5 minutes. Transfer the cherries and any remaining liquid to a food processor, add the vanilla, and process into a puree. Reserve 2 tablespoons of the puree at room temperature for the buttercream. In a small bowl, mix the remaining puree with the milk and set aside.

To make the cake, sift together the flour, baking powder, salt, and baking soda in a small bowl, then whisk the mixture by hand to ensure that the ingredients are well mixed.

In the bowl of a stand mixer fitted with the paddle attachment, cream the butter and sugar on medium-high speed until fluffy, about 5 minutes. As you make the batter, stop the mixer frequently and scrape the paddle and the sides of the bowl with a rubber spatula. With your mixer on low speed, drizzle the oil into the bowl until combined. Blend in the egg whites two at a time, adding the next two as soon as the previous two have disappeared into the batter. With the mixer on low speed, add the flour mixture in three parts, alternating with the cherry-milk mixture in two parts, beginning and ending with the flour. After each addition, mix until just barely blended and stop and scrape the bowl. Stop the mixer before the last

continued

of the flour has been incorporated and complete the blending by hand with a rubber spatula to ensure you do not overbeat the batter.

Divide the batter evenly among the prepared pans (there will be approximately 1 pound 2 ounces per pan) and bake in the middle of the oven until the cakes are slightly golden and the centers spring back when lightly touched, 30 to 32 minutes. Cool the cakes in their pans on a wire rack for 30 minutes. Flip the cakes out of the pans, leaving on the parchment paper until you assemble the cake. Let them continue to cool on the rack, top sides up, until they reach room temperature.

To assemble the cake, lay one of the cakes top side up on a serving plate. Using a metal spatula, frost the top with $1/3$ cup of ganache, spreading it to just shy of the cake's edge. Place the cake in the refrigerator for 5 minutes to firm up the ganache. Take it out and spread 1 cup of the buttercream on top of the ganached cake, taking it to the edge of the cake (you'll completely cover the ganache). Align the second cake top side up on top of the buttercream and spread it with another $1/3$ cup of ganache, chilling it again for 5 minutes to firm up. Spread another 1 cup of buttercream on top of the ganached cake, then stack the last layer of cake (also top side up) on top. Look for any buttercream that may have oozed out between the layers and spread it along the sides of the cake. Apply a thin layer of buttercream all over the cake to create a "crumb coat." Place the cake in the refrigerator until the frosting is firm, about 10 minutes. Take it out and finish the cake by frosting it with the remaining buttercream (for additional guidance on how to frost a cake, see page 10).

This cake keeps for up to 3 days in an airtight container at a cool room temperature.

TO MAKE CHERRY CHIP CUPCAKES, distribute the batter evenly by scooping $1/3$ cup ($2^1/4$ ounces) into each of 24 cupcake wells, either greased or lined with papers. Bake for 20 to 22 minutes. Frost the cupcakes with Dreamy Vanilla Frosting (page 156).

Blackout Cake

This is my tribute to Ebinger's Blackout Cake, which I have sadly never eaten (one of my life's few regrets!). I was two years old in 1972 when the Ebinger Baking Company in Brooklyn closed, and the genuine namesake cake was never baked again. The intense pudding-filled, all-chocolate cake coated with cake crumbs has taken on mythological proportions over the past forty years, as demonstrated by the numerous attempts to replicate it. Here is my version, which I hope does the original justice. I've included a recipe for chocolate shortbread cookies, which I use in place of the cake crumbs, but any crispy chocolate cookies could work—you'll need about 4^1/$_2$ ounces of cookies (6 to 8 cookies) to make a cup of crumbs. Both the cookies and the pudding can be made in advance of the cake.

12 servings	bake time	pan
	28 to 32 minutes	Three 9 by 2-inch round cake pans, greased and bottoms lined with parchment paper circles

CHOCOLATE SHORTBREAD COOKIES

3^1/$_2$ cups (1 pound 1 ^{1}/$_2$ ounces) all-purpose flour

^{1}/$_2$ cup (2^1/$_2$ ounces) rice flour

1 cup (4 ounces) lightly packed premium unsweetened Dutch-processed cocoa (see Cocoa Confusion, page 35)

2 cups (14 ounces) sugar

2 cups (1 pound) unsalted butter, at room temperature

^{3}/$_4$ teaspoon fine sea salt

1 tablespoon pure vanilla extract

If you are going to use store-bought cookies for your cookie crumbs, skip to the instructions for making the pudding, below. To make the cookies, combine the flours, and the cocoa in a bowl and whisk together. In the bowl of a stand mixer fitted with the paddle attachment, mix the sugar, butter, and salt at low speed until fully combined but not yet light and fluffy. Stir in the vanilla and scrape down the sides of bowl. Add the flour-cocoa mixture in two additions, still mixing at low speed, scraping down the bowl between each addition. Fully incorporate the flour but take care not to overmix.

Dump the dough onto a work surface and divide it into two pieces. Place each piece on a piece of parchment paper measuring 12 by 16 inches. Shape each piece of dough into a log about 12 inches long, then fold the parchment over the dough and roll the log back and forth. The parchment paper will help to smooth out the dough and make the log an even diameter. Transfer both logs to a baking sheet and refrigerate until firm, about 2 hours.

Center on oven rack and preheat the oven to 350°F.

Slice each log into ^{1}/$_2$-inch-thick slices and arrange the cookies on a baking sheet 1 inch apart. Bake until the cookies are firm in the center, 18 to 20 minutes. Let cool. Stored in an airtight container at room temperature, the cookies keep for up to 7 days. You can also freeze the unbaked logs, well wrapped, for up to 2 months. This amount of dough makes about 4 dozen cookies; you'll only need 6 to 8 cookies for the cake.

continued

PUDDING

1¹/₃ cups half-and-half

1¹/₃ cups (9²/₃ ounces) sugar

1¹/₂ cups whole milk

6 ounces unsweetened chocolate, chopped (about 1¹/₄ cups)

¹/₄ cup (1 ounce) cornstarch

1¹/₂ tablespoons lightly-packed premium unsweetened Dutch-processed cocoa (see Cocoa Confusion, page 35)

¹/₂ teaspoon fine sea salt

4 egg yolks

4 tablespoons (2 ounces) cold unsalted butter, cut into cubes

1 tablespoon pure vanilla extract

CAKE

³/₄ cup boiling water

³/₄ cup (3 ounces) lightly packed premium unsweetened Dutch-processed cocoa (see Cocoa Confusion, page 35)

³/₄ cup (6³/₄ ounces) full-fat sour cream

1 tablespoon pure vanilla extract

2 cups (10 ounces) all-purpose flour

³/₄ teaspoon baking soda

¹/₂ teaspoon fine sea salt

³/₄ cup (6 ounces) unsalted butter, at room temperature

2 cups (15 ounces) firmly packed brown sugar

³/₄ cup (5¹/₄ ounces) granulated sugar

3 eggs, at room temperature

To make the pudding, combine 1 cup of the half-and-half, 1 cup of the sugar, all the milk, and the chocolate in a saucepan over medium heat. Stir the mixture occasionally until the chocolate has melted and then turn the heat to low. In a separate bowl, whisk together the cornstarch, cocoa, salt, and the remaining ¹/₃ cup of sugar, then whisk in the remaining ¹/₃ cup of half-and-half and the egg yolks. Slowly whisk in about a third of the hot liquid into the yolk mixture. Pour this mixture back into the saucepan and cook over medium-low heat, whisking steadily, until the mixture begins to thicken and has bubbled for roughly 1 minute (you will need to stop whisking for a moment to check if it is bubbling). Strain the mixture through a fine mesh sieve into a shallow bowl and whisk in the butter and vanilla until the butter melts. Place a piece of plastic wrap directly on the surface of the pudding and refrigerate until cool. The pudding can be made up to 1 day ahead.

To make the cake, center an oven rack and preheat the oven to 350°F.

Whisk together the boiling water and cocoa in a small bowl. Blend in the sour cream and vanilla, and set aside.

Sift together the flour, baking soda, and salt in a bowl, then whisk the mixture by hand to ensure that the ingredients are well mixed.

In the bowl of a stand mixer fitted with the paddle attachment, cream the butter and sugars together on medium-high speed until fluffy, about 5 minutes. As you make the batter, stop the mixer frequently and scrape the paddle and the sides of the bowl with a rubber spatula. Blend in the eggs one at a time, adding the next one as soon as the previous one has disappeared into the batter. With the mixer on low speed, add the flour mixture in three parts, alternating with the cocoa mixture in two parts, beginning and ending with the flour. After each addition, mix until just barely blended and stop and scrape the bowl. Stop the mixer before the last of the flour has been incorporated and complete the blending by hand with a rubber spatula to ensure you do not overbeat the batter.

Divide the batter evenly among the prepared pans (there will be approximately 1 pound 3 ounces per pan) and smooth the tops. Bake in the middle of the oven until the centers are just barely firm when lightly touched, 28 to 32 minutes. Cool on a rack for 30 minutes before removing from the pans. Take extra care when removing the cakes from the pans, as they are fragile and could crack. Leave the parchment paper on until you assemble the cake. Continue to cool the cakes, top side up, on a rack until they reach room temperature.

To assemble the cake, put 4^1/$_2$ ounces of the cookies into a sealed plastic bag with the air pressed out and smash them with a rolling pin; you should end up with about 1 cup of crumbs. Spread 1^1/$_2$ cups of the pudding on one layer, top it with another layer and spread another 1^1/$_2$ cups on top of that layer, and align the third layer on top of the cake. "Frost" the cake with the remainder of the pudding by spreading a thin coat of pudding on the sides and mounding most of the pudding on top. Last, lightly press the cookie crumbs into the sides and top of the cake to completely coat the cake with crumbs.

Because of the pudding, this cake needs to be kept chilled until 1 hour before serving. It should return to the refrigerator within an hour or two if you are lucky enough to have any leftovers.

The Magic of Cornstarch

Cornstarch is a thickening agent. It needs to come to a full boil before any thickening will begin. After boiling for one full minute, the starch particles will have swelled to capacity, which is what causes any mixture they are in to thicken. Overcooking a thickened custard may cause the mixture to thin when it cools, however, so be sure to remove the custard from the heat once it has thickened.

Gingerbread Icebox Cake with Mascarpone Mousse

Store-bought confections like Tastykakes, Entenmann's, and Ivins' were treats we could not find on the grocery store shelves as kids growing up in rural Vermont. Instead, we waited eagerly for a visit from my grandmother, who would drive eight hours north from Philadelphia with her trunk packed full of boxed goodies. My oldest brother always settled into the Ivins' Famous Spiced Wafers, which appeared every autumn at the Acme grocery chain in Philly. This cake was created with the spice flavor of those wafers in mind (never fear if you don't have a source for Ivins', as this recipe uses homemade spice cookies, rolled as thin as possible to resemble wafers). Note that this cake needs to rest overnight to allow the flavors to meld and the cookies to soften.

8 to 10 servings	bake time/wafers	pan
	12 to 14 minutes	A baking sheet or two, either lightly greased or lined with parchment paper

WAFERS

4³/₄ cups (23³/₄ ounces) all-purpose flour

1 tablespoon ground ginger

1 tablespoon ground cinnamon

1 teaspoon ground cloves

³/₄ teaspoon baking soda

¹/₄ teaspoon baking powder

¹/₂ teaspoon fine sea salt

³/₄ cup (6 ounces) unsalted butter, at room temperature

³/₄ cup (5²/₃ ounces) firmly packed brown sugar

2 eggs

³/₄ cup (9 ounces) unsulfured blackstrap molasses

MOUSSE

1 pound mascarpone, cold

1¹/₂ cups heavy cream, cold

¹/₃ cup (2¹/₃ ounces) sugar

2 tablespoons pure vanilla extract, or ¹/₄ cup brandy

To make the wafers, center an oven rack and preheat the oven to 350°F.

Sift together the flour, ginger, cinnamon, cloves, baking soda, baking powder, and salt into a bowl, then whisk the mixture by hand to ensure that the ingredients are well mixed.

In the bowl of a stand mixer fitted with the paddle attachment, mix the butter and brown sugar on medium speed until well combined. Add the eggs one at a time, scraping down the sides and bottom of the bowl between additions. Blend in the molasses. Add the dry ingredients all at once and combine on low speed, scraping down the bowl as needed to create a unified dough. Divide the dough in four quarters and shape each piece into a rough rectangle about 1 inch thick. Wrap each piece tightly in plastic wrap and refrigerate the dough until it is firm enough to roll out, about 2 hours.

On a lightly floured surface, roll out the dough with a rolling pin to ¹/₈ inch thick or even a bit thinner (use a ruler; you can never go too thin, but you will need to reduce your baking time if you roll the dough thinner than ¹/₈ inch). Using a 2¹/₂-inch round cookie cutter, cut out disks and place them 1 inch apart on the prepared baking sheet. Gather up the scraps and reroll. If the dough gets too warm and hard to handle, pop it back in the refrigerator to firm up before continuing. You will need

continued

70 wafers to assemble the cake. If you have extra dough, use it to cut some festive cookies to embellish the top of the cake, or chill it to make more gingerbread wafers later; the dough will keep in the refrigerator for up to 5 days or in the freezer for 2 months.

Bake the wafers until golden around the edges and firm on top, 12 to 14 minutes. Let the wafers cool on their baking sheet until cool enough to handle, then remove them to a wire rack to cool completely.

Once the wafers are baked, make the mascarpone mousse. Place a mixing bowl or the bowl of a stand mixer and its whisk attachment in the freezer for 5 minutes to chill. Blend the mascarpone, cream, and sugar in the cold bowl on low speed until combined. Increase the speed to medium high and whip just until the cream becomes thick and fluffy and holds a stiff peak (warning: overmixing will cause the contents to curdle.) Blend in the vanilla or brandy on low speed until just incorporated.

To assemble the cake, spread about 2 tablespoons of the cream on a flat serving plate. Arrange 6 wafers touching side by side in a circle plus 1 wafer in the middle. Spread a heaping $1/2$ cup of mousse atop the wafers, almost covering them but leaving a smidge of room at the edge of the circle. Repeat with another 7 wafers and more mousse, offsetting the wafers from the previous layer so they do not stack right on top of each other. Repeat until you have ten layers of wafers staggered with ten layers of mousse (not counting your initial dollop on the plate), topping the last layer of wafers with all the mousse that is left in the bowl. Cover loosely with plastic wrap and refrigerate for at least 12 hours. Serve chilled, and if you made any decorative cookies, arrange them on the top.

This cake keeps for up to 3 days refrigerated in an airtight container.

Peppermint Patty Flourless Chocolate Cake

This flourless chocolate cake with a peppermint filling is my ode to the candy world. Candy production (including York Peppermint Patties, one of my favorites!) went into high gear in the 1940s and 1950s, and not long after, peppermint candy started showing up in cake recipes. This is a cake that tastes like the candy but doesn't actually call for any candy in the ingredients. This flourless chocolate cake needs to be baked one day ahead of when you will serve it. A word of warning: peppermint oil is very concentrated, and a little goes a long way. Feel free to add extra oil, drop by drop, if you want to "get the sensation!"

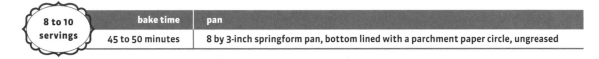

8 to 10 servings	bake time	pan
	45 to 50 minutes	8 by 3-inch springform pan, bottom lined with a parchment paper circle, ungreased

CAKE

8 ounces bittersweet chocolate, chips or chopped

1/2 cup (4 ounces) unsalted butter, cut into cubes

1 tablespoon pure vanilla extract

6 eggs, separated, at room temperature

1/2 cup (3 1/2 ounces) plus 2 tablespoons sugar

1/8 teaspoon fine sea salt

FILLING

8 ounces premium white chocolate, chopped

2/3 cup heavy cream

1 teaspoon pure vanilla extract

1/4 teaspoon peppermint oil, or 1 tablespoon peppermint extract

3/4 cup Chocolate Ganache (page 146)

Center an oven rack and preheat the oven to 350°F.

To make the cake, place the bittersweet chocolate and butter in a bowl set over simmering water, stirring occasionally until melted. Remove from the heat and stir in the vanilla. Set the chocolate mixture aside, stirring occasionally until it is cool but still fluid.

Using a stand mixer fitted with the whisk attachment, beat the eggs yolks on low speed to break them up, then gradually add 1/2 cup of the sugar. Increase the speed to high and beat until the mixture is thick and fluffy, about 6 minutes. Remove the yolks to a mixing bowl and fold the cooled chocolate mixture into the yolks by hand with a rubber spatula.

Thoroughly wash and dry both the stand mixer bowl and the whisk attachment and fit both to the mixer. Whip the egg whites and salt on low speed until frothy. Raise the speed to medium-high and beat until the whites just begin to hold their shape. Slowly add the remaining 2 tablespoons of sugar and continue whipping until the whites hold medium-soft—not yet firm—peaks. Gently fold one third of the whites into the batter to lighten it up, then fold the rest of the whites into the batter until just thoroughly combined.

Pour the batter into the pan and place it in the middle of the oven. It's a bit tricky to know when a flourless cake is done, but here are some good signs to follow: the cake will crack a bit on the surface, lose its shine, and be firm to the touch even though inside the cracks, the cake will not look baked through and it will wiggle a bit when you jiggle the pan. It should take 45 to 50 minutes to bake this cake. Remove the cake to a wire rack to cool to room temperature, about 1 hour. (The cake will sink slightly in the middle as it cools, creating the perfect space for the filling.)

To make the filling, put the white chocolate in a small heat-resistant bowl. Heat the cream in a small saucepan over medium heat until the cream begins to simmer but not boil. Promptly pour the cream over the white chocolate and swirl the bowl so that all the chocolate is coated with the hot cream. Cover the bowl with a lid to trap the heat. Let it sit for 5 minutes, then remove the lid and whisk the mixture together until smooth. Whisk in the vanilla extract and peppermint oil. (Use caution when handling the oil, as it is very strong.) With the cake still in its pan, pour the filling onto the center of the cake, filling up the sunken part just to the top. Carefully place the cake in the refrigerator until the top has set, then cover it with plastic wrap and chill overnight.

To finish the cake, insert a thin knife or a metal spatula around the edge of the pan to free the cake from the sides and then remove the sides of the springform pan. Carefully remove the parchment paper from the bottom of the cake and place the cake on a serving platter.

Make the ganache, and while it's still warm, pour it over the top of the cake and filling, artfully allowing some to drip down the sides. Use a thin metal spatula or the back of a spoon to make a swirl or two in the ganache, reminiscent of the top of a peppermint patty. To cut the cake, warm a long, thin knife under hot water before slicing each piece.

Under a cake dome, this cake keeps at cool room temperature for up to 3 days.

Fillings, Frostings, and Icings

I'm a true believer in the notion that the frosting should taste as good as the cake. Life is too short for sickly sweet icing and greasy tasteless frosting. In this chapter, you'll find lots of decadent chocolate frostings, from ganache to fudge to malted milk, as well as divine silky buttercreams with flavors made from vanilla beans, raspberry puree, and espresso. Though the recipes in this book suggest certain frostings to complement particular cakes, the recipes can become entirely new creations when you mix and match the cakes and the frostings. Look for the sidebars that suggest cake combinations for some of the most versatile frostings.

Chocolate Ganache

yield	note
Makes about 1½ cups (enough to lightly glaze or frost an 8- or 9-inch cake)	If you are using the ganache as a frosting (rather than a glaze), make it at least 2 or 3 hours before you'll need it, as it takes time to reach a spreading consistency.

1 or 1¼ cups heavy cream, depending on the type of chocolate

8 ounces semisweet or bittersweet chocolate, chopped or chips

Measure the chocolate into a small heat-resistant bowl. If you are using semisweet chocolate, use 1 cup of cream. If you are using bittersweet chocolate, use 1¼ cups of cream. Heat the cream in a saucepan over medium heat, stirring occasionally. When the cream begins to simmer, quickly remove the pot from the heat and pour it over the chocolate. Swirl the bowl to ensure that all the chocolate is coated with the hot cream.

Cover the bowl with a lid to trap the heat, and let it rest for 5 minutes. Remove the lid and begin to slowly whisk the mixture, starting with small circles in the middle and working your way outward until you have a smooth, glossy frosting.

If you intend to use the ganache as a glaze, let it cool at room temperature for about 30 minutes. Pour the liquid ganache over your cake while the ganache is still warm but not hot. If the ganache thickens too much, rewarm it by placing it over (not in) simmering water.

If you plan to use the ganache as a frosting (not a glaze), you can leave the ganache at room temperature, stirring occasionally, until it reaches spreading consistency. The time varies for this depending on your room temperature, but plan for 2 to 3 hours. Alternatively, you can pop it into the refrigerator to hurry this process, gently stirring it with a spatula every 10 minutes or so until it stiffens up to spreading consistency. If the ganache ever becomes too hard to spread, simply put it somewhere warm to soften.

Covered with plastic wrap at room temperature, this frosting keeps for up to 3 days.

Chocolate Infusion

You'll always find a large bowl of decadent ganache on the baker's table at Baker & Spice. When we make the Pink Cake (page 121) and Black & White Cake (page 123), we like to spread ganache thinly atop the cake layers before slathering on the buttercream.

Caramel Chocolate Ganache

yield	note
Makes just over 2 cups (enough to frost an 8- or 9-inch cake)	If you are using the ganache as a frosting (rather than a glaze), make it at least 2 or 3 hours before you'll need it, as it takes time to reach a spreading consistency.

8 ounces semisweet chocolate, chopped or chips

$1/2$ cup ($3^1/_2$ ounces) sugar

1 tablespoon water

1 teaspoon lemon juice

1 cup heavy cream

2 tablespoons unsalted butter, cut into small cubes

Put the chocolate into a small heat-resistant bowl and set aside.

Put the sugar, water, and lemon juice in a saucepan over medium heat and stir just until the sugar has dissolved (see Making Caramel, page 101). Put down your spoon and let the syrup come to a boil without stirring, occasionally washing down the sides of the pan with a pastry brush dipped in water. Cook the syrup until it turns a dark amber color. Swirl the pan to distribute the color and heat.

Once the syrup reaches the desired color, take the pan off the heat and pour in $^1/_3$ cup of the cream. Do this carefully, as the caramel is very hot and will bubble up when you add the cream. Once the bubbling subsides stir in the rest of the cream $^1/_3$ cup at a time, then stir in the butter a piece at a time. Place the pan back over medium heat and stir to combine all the ingredients. Once the ingredients are all incorporated into the caramel, pour it over the chocolate. Swirl the bowl so that the chocolate is completely coated with the warm caramel, then cover and let sit for 5 minutes. With a whisk, stir the mixture slowly, starting with small circles in the middle and working your way outward, whisking a bit more briskly as you go, until you have a smooth, glossy frosting. Leave the ganache on your kitchen counter, stirring now and then to help it cool, until it reaches spreading consistency, about 3 hours. If it stiffens up too much, simply put it someplace warmer than your counter.

Covered with plastic wrap at room temperature, this frosting keeps for up to 3 days.

Basic Buttercream and Variations

yield

Makes about 5 cups (enough to frost one 8- or 9-inch layer cake)

6 egg whites

1¼ cups (8¾ ounces) sugar

¼ teaspoon cream of tartar

2 cups (1 pound) unsalted butter, at room temperature, cut into small cubes

2 teaspoons pure vanilla extract

⅛ teaspoon fine sea salt

Using a hand whisk, whisk together the egg whites, sugar, and cream of tartar in the clean bowl of a stand mixer. Place the bowl over (not in) a saucepan of simmering water. The egg white mixture will be gloppy and thick, but as the mixture begins to warm up, it will become more fluid. Continue to gently whisk the mixture until it is very hot to the touch (130°F on a candy thermometer).

Move the bowl to the stand mixer and, using the whisk attachment, whip the whites on medium-high speed until they have tripled in volume and are thick and glossy and hold stiff peaks (like meringue), 3 to 4 minutes. Turn the mixer down to medium-low speed until the mixing bowl is just cool to the touch, 1 to 2 minutes. Kick the mixer back up to medium-high speed and add the butter one piece at a time, adding the next piece just as the previous one has been incorporated. Stop the mixer every so often to scrape down the escaping buttercream from the sides of the bowl. At some point, the buttercream will take on a curdled appearance; don't worry, this is normal. Just keep on mixing until it comes together. Once all the butter is incorporated and the frosting is fluffy and creamy, blend in the vanilla and salt until fully combined.

Covered with plastic wrap, buttercream will last 2 days at room temperature or 7 days in the refrigerator. If refrigerated, the buttercream must be brought to room temperature before you use it. Either way, the buttercream must be rewhipped—either by hand if kept at room temperature or with a mixer if refrigerated—before you frost a cake with it.

Buttercream Variations

CHERRY BUTTERCREAM: To the Basic Buttercream recipe above, add 2 tablespoons cherry puree reserved from the recipe for Cherry Chip Cake (page 133) and 2 to 3 tablespoons Kirschwasser (a colorless cherry brandy) at the end of the recipe with the vanilla and the salt.

CHOCOLATE BUTTERCREAM: Make the Basic Buttercream recipe. Melt 5 ounces of chopped bittersweet chocolate. Cool the chocolate until barely warm and melted, then stir it into a cup of buttercream. Add the chocolate mixture back into the buttercream and whip until combined.

COFFEE BUTTERCREAM: Make the Basic Buttercream recipe. Combine 1 tablespoon of instant espresso powder with 2 teaspoons of water. Add this espresso paste to the buttercream and whip until combined.

COFFEE WALNUT BUTTERCREAM: First, make a walnut-espresso paste: Puree 1 cup (4 ounces) of toasted chopped walnuts in a food processor until they just begin to form a paste. Add $^1/_4$ cup of corn syrup, $^1/_4$ cup of bourbon, and 2 tablespoons of instant espresso powder and blend until combined. Set aside. Make the Basic Buttercream, using 5 egg whites, $1^1/_4$ cups ($8^3/_4$ ounces) of sugar, $^1/_4$ teaspoon of cream of tartar, $1^1/_2$ cups (12 ounces) of room-temperature unsalted butter cut into 1-inch pieces, and $^1/_4$ teaspoon of fine sea salt (omit the vanilla). Add the walnut paste at the very end, when you add the salt.

LEMON BUTTERCREAM: Make the Basic Buttercream recipe. Add $^1/_2$ to $^3/_4$ cup of premade lemon curd to the finished buttercream and whip until combined.

RASPBERRY BUTTERCREAM: Mash and strain 4 cups (10 ounces) of raspberries, fresh or frozen, through a fine mesh sieve to catch the seeds. (If using frozen berries, measure them before thawing.) Discard the seeds and set aside the puree while you follow the method for making Basic Buttercream. Add the berry puree at the end of the recipe, with the vanilla and the salt.

VANILLA BEAN BUTTERCREAM: To the Basic Buttercream recipe, add both 1 extra teaspoon of vanilla and the seeds scraped from half a vanilla bean pod split lengthwise when adding the salt.

Beautiful Buttercream

Buttercream is a delicious alternative to that overly sweet frosting made with confectioners' sugar. It is light, silky smooth, and easy to work with. Don't despair if, as you make it, the frosting appears curdled; this is a natural step in the process. Just keep mixing, and all will be well in the end.

Malted Milk Chocolate Frosting

yield	note
Makes about 4 cups (enough to frost 24 cupcakes)	Make this recipe ahead of time, as it takes about 2 hours to chill to a spreading consistency.

12 ounces milk chocolate, chopped or chips

1 cup (5 ounces) malted milk powder

1 cup heavy cream

$1/2$ cup (4 ounces) unsalted butter, at room temperature, and cut into small cubes

Put the chocolate into the mixing bowl of a stand mixer. Put the malted milk powder into a small saucepan and whisk in the heavy cream $1/2$ cup at a time to prevent the malt from forming clumps. Place the saucepan on the stove over medium heat, stirring often, until the cream begins to bubble around the edge of the pan. (Malted milk powder is essentially sugar, so it will burn unless you keep stirring the cream.) Pour the cream over the chocolate and swirl the bowl so that all the chocolate is coated with the hot cream. Place a lid or plastic wrap over the bowl and let it sit for 5 minutes. Remove the lid or wrap and slowly begin to whisk the mixture, starting with small circles in the middle and working your way outward until you have a smooth, glossy frosting. Cover the bowl with plastic wrap and place in the refrigerator to chill for about 2 hours.

To finish the frosting, remove the bowl from the refrigerator and fit it into the stand mixer. Beat the butter into the frosting with the whisk attachment: begin adding a few butter pieces on low speed, then add more as soon as the butter has been incorporated into the frosting. Once the butter has all been added, mix the frosting on medium-high speed until it is thick and creamy. If the frosting seems too soft, just pop it back into the refrigerator to chill before frosting the cupcakes.

Covered with plastic wrap at room temperature, this frosting keeps for up to 3 days. Refrigerated, it lasts for 7 days.

Fudge Frosting

	yield	note
	Makes about 3¼ cups (enough to fill and frost one 8- or 9-inch layer cake)	Make this recipe ahead of time, as it takes approximately 1 hour to reach a spreading consistency.

1 pound semisweet chocolate, chopped or chips

2 cups heavy cream

½ cup (3¾ ounces) firmly packed dark brown sugar

Put the chocolate into a medium heat-resistant bowl. Combine the cream and brown sugar in a saucepan over medium heat, stirring occasionally. When the cream begins to simmer, quickly remove the pan from the heat and pour the liquid over the chocolate. Swirl the bowl to confirm that all the chocolate is coated with the hot cream. Place a lid or plastic wrap over the bowl an letit sit for 5 minutes. Remove the lid or wrap and slowly begin to whisk the mixture, starting with small circles in the middle and working your way outward until you have a smooth, glossy frosting.

You now have two choices depending on your time: the quickest method is to put the frosting in the refrigerator and gently stir it with a spatula every 10 minutes until it stiffens up to spreading consistency; this will take less than an hour (caveat: the frosting runs the risk of getting too hard, in which case you would need to take it out of the refrigerator and put it somewhere warm to soften). Alternatively, just leave the frosting on your kitchen counter, stirring occasionally, until it reaches spreading consistency, about an hour. If it stiffens up too much, simply put it someplace warmer than your counter.

Covered with plastic wrap at room temperature, this frosting keeps for up to 3 days.

A Very Versatile Frosting

This frosting is basically a chocolate ganache, but I've added brown sugar to lend it a fudge flavor. Pair this frosting with any of the following:

Wacky Cake (page 21)

Mississippi Mud Cupcakes (page 55)

Shinny Cake (page 88)

Watergate Cake (page 99)

Goober Cake (page 111)

Cherry Chip Cupcakes (page 134)

Mascarpone Cream Cheese Frosting

Makes about 3 cups (enough to fill and top but not completely frost an 8- or 9-inch layer cake)

8 ounces cream cheese, at room
temperature

8 ounces mascarpone, cold

$1/2$ cup heavy cream, cold

$1/3$ cup ($2^{1}/2$ ounces) sugar

1 tablespoon pure vanilla extract

Using a stand mixer fitted with the paddle attachment, beat the cream cheese until it is uniform in texture. Add the mascarpone, cream, and sugar. Beat on low speed until combined, scraping the sides of the bowl well to ensure all the ingredients are incorporated. Kick the mixer up to high speed and blend the frosting for about 1 minute or until it looks creamy and thick. Turn down to low speed, add the vanilla, and mix just until blended.

This frosting keeps in the refrigerator for up to 5 days. If the frosting is refrigerated before you use it, it will need to be softened slightly by blending with a rubber spatula until smooth.

Decadent Duos

For a delicious combination, pair the Mascarpone Cream Cheese Frosting or the basic Cream Cheese Frosting (on the next page) with any of the following cakes:

Banana Cake (page 93)

Carrot Cake (page 94)

Red Velvet Cake (page 96)

Jam Cake (page 103)

Italian Cream Cake (page 105)

Cream Cheese Frosting

yield
Makes about 2¹/₂ cups (enough to lightly fill and top but not completely frost an 8- or 9-inch layer cake)

12 ounces cream cheese, cold, cut into 1-inch cubes

¹/₂ cup (4 ounces) unsalted butter, at room temperature, cut into small cubes

¹/₂ cup (3¹/₂ ounces) sugar

2 teaspoons pure vanilla extract

Put the cream cheese in the bowl of a stand mixer fitted with the paddle attachment and blend on medium speed to soften. While mixing on medium speed, gradually add the butter pieces and continue beating until all the butter is incorporated. Next, add the sugar and vanilla and continue mixing on medium speed until the frosting is well blended and has a smooth texture.

This frosting keeps in the refrigerator for up to 7 days. If refrigerated, the frosting will need to be brought back to room temperature and rewhipped before using.

Maple Cream Cheese Frosting

yield	note
Makes about 3 cups (enough to fill and top but not completely frost an 8- or 9-inch layer cake)	For this recipe to be foolproof, stay away from artisan cream cheese and stick with the more common name brands (they don't curdle when whipped). Also, use grade B maple syrup, which has a strong maple flavor with caramel undertones.

1 cup (8 ounces) unsalted butter, at room temperature, cut into small cubes

1 pound cream cheese, at room temperature, cut into 1-inch cubes

1 teaspoon instant espresso powder

1 tablespoon pure vanilla extract

²/₃ cup pure maple syrup

In the bowl of a stand mixer fitted with the paddle attachment, beat the butter on medium speed for about 1 minute, until it is smooth. Add the cream cheese and continue beating until the frosting is smooth and lump-free, about 1 more minute. Dissolve the espresso powder in the vanilla and blend this mixture into the frosting. Blend in the maple syrup. Continue mixing on medium-high speed, scraping the bowl as necessary to rid the frosting of stubborn lumps, until the frosting is well blended and has a smooth texture. If the frosting is too soft to work with, just pop it in the refrigerator to firm up.

This frosting keeps in the refrigerator for up to 7 days. If refrigerated, the frosting will need to be brought back to room temperature and rewhipped before using.

Brown Butter Icing

yield	note
Makes about 2 ¼ cups (enough to ice an 8- or 9-inch cake)	Make this recipe ahead of time, as it takes time to reach a spreading consistency.

4 cups (1 pound) sifted confectioners' sugar

1 cup (8 ounces) unsalted butter, cut into small cubes

¹/₂ cup heavy cream, plus a little more to thin as needed

1 tablespoon pure vanilla extract

Pinch of fine sea salt

Put the sugar in a medium mixing bowl and set aside. Melt the butter in a small saucepan over medium heat. Using a pan with a light-colored bottom will help you keep track of the color. Let the color of the butter darken from lemony to golden brown (swirl the pan occasionally to ensure even heating). Once the butter is dark brown and you begin to smell a nutty aroma, remove the pan from the heat. You can either pour the butter off carefully to leave behind the milk solids that have collected on the bottom of the pan, or you can keep and use the butter solids. Either way, pour the butter into the bowl containing the confectioners' sugar and add the cream, vanilla, and salt. Whisk until smooth. As the butter cools, the icing will become firmer. If using the icing as a glaze, use it immediately. If you plan to use the icing as a frosting, allow it to cool to a good spreading consistency.

Peanut Butter Frosting

yield
Makes about 2¹/₂ cups (enough to fill and top but not completely frost an 8- or 9-inch layer cake)

6 tablespoons (3 ounces) unsalted butter, at room temperature, cut into small cubes

¹/₂ cup (5 ounces) natural crunchy salted peanut butter, at room temperature

2¹/₂ cups (10 ounces) sifted confectioners' sugar

¹/₂ cup heavy cream

1 teaspoon pure vanilla extract

In the bowl of a stand mixer fitted with the paddle attachment, beat the butter and peanut butter on medium speed until smooth. Add the confectioners' sugar, cream, and vanilla and continue beating until the frosting is light and creamy, about 3 minutes. Scrape the sides and bottom of the bowl, as well as the paddle, as often as necessary to incorporate all the ingredients. This frosting keeps at room temperature for up to 3 days or can be stored in the refrigerator for up to 7 days. If refrigerated, the frosting will need to be brought back to room temperature and rewhipped before using.

Marshmallow Frosting

yield	note
Makes about 6 cups (enough to generously frost 24 cupcakes)	You must use a candy thermometer for this recipe!

1 cup (7 ounces) sugar

¹⁄₄ teaspoon cream of tartar

¹⁄₂ cup water

4 egg whites

¹⁄₈ teaspoon fine sea salt

2 teaspoons pure vanilla extract

Combine the sugar, cream of tartar, and water in a small saucepan that has a tight-fitting lid. Place the pan, uncovered, over medium heat. Bring the mixture to a boil, then cover and cook for 2 minutes. (Covering in this manner allows the steam to wash down the sides of pan, which will prevent any sugar crystals from forming.) Uncover the saucepan and continue to boil until the sugar syrup reaches the soft-ball stage, 242°F on a candy thermometer.

While the syrup is heating to the desired temperature, combine the egg whites with the salt in the clean bowl of a stand mixer fitted with the whisk attachment and beat beginning at low speed and gradually increasing to medium-high speed. Beat the whites just until soft peaks form. Timing is crucial at this point in the game; if the syrup is close to reaching 242°F, continue whipping the whites to firm peaks. If the syrup is not this warm yet, let the whites wait at the soft-peak stage before whipping them into firm peaks as the syrup approaches the desired temperature.

Once the sugar syrup has reached 242°F and the egg whites are whipped to firm peaks, run the mixer at medium-high speed and begin slowly pouring the syrup down the inside of the bowl (try to keep the syrup from hitting the whisk attachment or you'll have quite a mess on your hands). Continue whipping until the frosting becomes thick and holds stiff peaks, about 5 minutes. Add the vanilla and whip to combine.

This frosting should be used immediately.

Dreamy Vanilla Frosting

¼ cup (1¼ ounces) all-purpose flour

1 cup half-and-half or whole milk

1 cup (8 ounces) unsalted butter, at room temperature, cut into small cubes

1 cup (7 ounces) sugar

⅛ teaspoon fine sea salt

1 tablespoon pure vanilla extract

Sift the flour into a small bowl. Whisk ¼ cup of the half-and-half into the flour until smooth. Whisk in the remaining ¾ cup of the half-and-half and transfer to a small saucepan. Bring the mixture to a simmer over medium heat, whisking all the while. Cook the mixture at a simmer for about 30 seconds, stirring with a wooden spoon, until it begins to thicken and becomes a paste. Remove the mixture from the heat and transfer to a small bowl. Press a piece of plastic wrap directly on the surface of the mixture. Cool to room temperature. (Placing the bowl in the refrigerator for 20 minutes helps speed up the process.)

Combine the butter, sugar, and salt in the bowl of a stand mixer fitted with the paddle attachment and beat on high speed until fluffy, about 5 minutes, scraping the bowl once or twice during this process. Add the cooled milk mixture to the bowl and beat on high speed until fluffy and light, 3 to 5 minutes. Add the vanilla and blend to combine.

Covered with plastic wrap at room temperature, this frosting keeps for 2 days. Refrigerated, it lasts for 10 days. This frosting will need to be rewhipped at room temperature before using.

Dreamy Duets

This creamy frosting is a great alternative to traditional buttercream. Try it with any of the following:

Mississippi Mud Cupcakes (page 55)

Banana Cake (page 93)

Carrot Cake (page 94)

Red Velvet Cake (page 96)

Old Vermont Burnt Sugar Cake (page 127)

Cherry Chip Cupcakes (page 134)

BIBLIOGRAPHY

Anderson, Jean. *The American Century Cookbook.* New York: Clarkson Potter, 1997.

Beard, James. *James Beard's American Cookery.* Boston: Little, Brown and Co., 1972.

Corriher, Shirley O. *BakeWise.* New York: Scribner, 2008.

Daley, Regan. *In the Sweet Kitchen.* New York: Artisan, 2001.

General Mills. *Betty Crocker's Picture Cook Book*, second ed. New York: McGraw-Hill, 1956.

Glabau, Charles A. "Year 'Round Recipes," *Bakers Weekly,* 1937.

Glabau, Charles A. "Year 'Round Recipes," *Bakers Weekly,* 1953.

King, Daisy. *Recipes from Miss Daisy's.* Franklin, TN: Miss Daisy's Tearoom, 1973.

Nichols, Nell. *Farm Journal's Country Cookbook.* Garden City, NY: Doubleday & Company, Inc., 1959.

Sax, Richard. *Classic Home Desserts.* Shelburne, VT: Chapter Publishing, Ltd., 1994.

Scherber, Amy, and Toy Kim Dupree. *The Sweeter Side of Amy's Bread.* Hoboken, NJ: John Wiley & Sons, Inc., 2008.

Schreiber, Cory, and Julie Richardson. *Rustic Fruit Desserts.* Berkeley, CA: Ten Speed Press, 2009.

Zenker, John J. "Fine Cakes from Two Basic Formulas," *Baking Industry Magazine*, 1967.

INDEX

Copyright © 2012 by Julie Richardson

Photographs copyright © 2012 by Erin Kunkel

All rights reserved.

Published in the United States by Ten Speed Press, an imprint of the Crown Publishing Group,
a division of Random House, Inc., New York.

www.crownpublishing.com

www.tenspeed.com

Ten Speed Press and the Ten Speed Press colophon are registered trademarks of Random House, Inc.

Library of Congress Cataloging-in-Publicaion Data

Richardson, Julie, 1970–

   Vintage cakes : timeless recipes for cupcakes, flips, rolls, layer, angel, bundt, chiffon, and icebox cakes
for today's sweet tooth / by Julie Richardson.

       p. cm.

   Includes bibliographical references and index.

1. Cake. I. Title.

  TX771.R527 2012

  641.86'53—dc23

            2011041262

ISBN: 978-1-60774-102-2

eISBN: 978-1-60774-103-9

Cover and text design by Toni Tajima

Food styling by Robyn Valarik

Prop styling by Ethel Brennan

10 9 8 7 6 5 4 3 2 1

Printed in China

First Edition